COSMIC INNER SEEING

A MEMOIR

DR. CYNTHIA MILLER

Gold Dot
Publishing

Gold Dot Publishing
Copyright © 2020 by Dr. Cynthia Miller

Previously published as *Unseen Connections: A Memoir from Pain and Violence to Joy*. All rights reserved. No part of this book may be reproduced in any form or by any electronic or mechanical means, including information storage and retrieval systems, without written permission from the author, except for the use of brief quotations in a book review.

The processes in this book are not meant to diagnose, treat, or cure any condition. Please note that this book is not a substitute for medical help. Please consult with your health care professional regarding any medical or psychological conditions.

All of the information in this book is published in good faith and for general information purposes only. There is no warranty for the completeness, reliability, and accuracy of this information. Any action that you take based on the information in this book is strictly at your own risk, and we will not be liable for any losses and damages in connection with the information in this book. We are not responsible for your actions.

Revised August 2025

golddotpublishing.store
ISBN: 978-0-9887763-9-5

Cover: NASA photo, design Dr. Cynthia Miller
Author Photos: Dr. Cynthia Miller
Photographs, drawings, and text copyright Dr. Cynthia Miller
© 2025 Dr. Cynthia Miller

To all the brave, courageous souls who are here on Earth to create a new humanity and reality ~ the outcasts, weirdos, misfits, magical beings, angels, star seeds, multidimensional visionaries, artists, and more...

ALSO BY DR. CYNTHIA MILLER

Inner Evolution: Remembering Your Power

The Art of Radical Gratitude

*I Am Worthy: Ignite Your Feminine Power -
Self-Help Adult Coloring Book*

CONTENTS

Authors Note   ix

BOOK 1
Cosmic Secrets

VW Space Odyssey	3
Hiding in Plain Sight	7
Why Do People Kill Each Other?	15
Train Hopping in Iran	19
Swiss Boarding School	31
Temple Carvings and Locust Invasions	39
Love, Drugs, and Hippies	47
I've got the Sugar Blues	53
Tunnel of Luminous Light	59
Bolt of Light	63

BOOK 2
Exploring the Unknown

Spontaneous Awakening	67
Endings	71
Mt. Everest Clean-Up Trek	75
African Elephants in Kathmandu	83
The River	87
The Grand Adventure	95
Moonlight Ascent of Mt. Sopris	107
Ph.D. Cellular Transformation	113
Healing Angels	119
Dad and Quantum Physics	127
River of Souls	131
Choose Me	137
Fourth of July Fireworks	139
Shaman's Drumbeat	143
Bright Red Apple	147
Cobras and Caves	151
No Mind	165

Seattle Needles	171
Ashes	177
The Manila Envelope	179
Exploding Orgasmic Bombs	189
Stripped to the Bone	191
Radical Gratitude	197
The Radiance Project	205
Hibakusha	213
The Galactic Petri Dish Experiment	221

BOOK 3
Multi-Dimensional Awakening

Weaving the Pieces Together	231
It's Your Turn!	235
Acknowledgments	239
Glossary	241
About the Author	245

AUTHORS NOTE

Dear Reader,

Cosmic Inner Seeing: A Memoir is a revision of *Unseen Connections: A Memoir from Pain and Violence to Joy*. In addition to adding juicy bits to various chapters, I've removed the final chapters and added a new ending.

I'm one of the first-born of the nuclear age. I remember the day well when my Dad came home from building the world's first hydrogen bomb. I was five years old. I couldn't comprehend why people hate and kill each other. That day signaled my life's trajectory.

My twisting life path has been arduous and triumphant. Incredible highs, death-gripping terror, and miraculous adventures open

Authors Note

the way to a profound discovery about how to shift the core of violence, fear, and hatred into love and joy.

This epic adventure brings together the macro and the micro, world events pinpointed in one life—the evolution from unconsciousness to consciousness, from trauma to healing, from victim to self-discovery, and from horror to awakening.

My life has been very unusual; both the external events and the inner workings are complex, reaching extremes of higher heights and much greater depths than most people dare to explore. At times, it morphs into a sci-fi movie.

I must admit that while many memories were burned clearly into my mind with minute detail, some of the events have blurred over the past seventy-something years. Most of the names and identities have been changed to protect people's privacy. All the events in the book are spontaneous; none are drug-induced.

This multidimensional memoir exposes you to layers of reality you may not be familiar with - subatomic particles, cells, DNA, and neural programs, along with the stratum of angels, cosmic forces, and divine soul essence. Some of what I write is bizarre, perhaps activating suppressed, long-forgotten memories of your own. Deep down, you may be triggered to see an extraordinary reality. I invite you to crack open and peek beyond the veil of your current existence.

How you understand this book will depend on your reality. Many think there is only one reality, and if we differ from that existence, then something is wrong; there is an internal flaw. I believe we each live in distinct worlds influenced by our inherited and childhood programs, our experiences, and the collective unconscious.

I invite you to read with an open mind and heart and explore what's hidden deep inside, covering your gifts and vision. Allow yourself to awaken some deeper unconscious or intuitive insights about who you are and your sense of reality. You may experience discomfort, ease, or relief. Deep inside, you may resonate with the truth of what I'm saying.

While writing my life story, I discovered a model for evolving into happiness, fulfillment, and awakening. The new reality we are conceiving is a tremendous leap in human consciousness, shifting from fear, victim consciousness, and violence into love, generosity, and gratitude.

New ideas tend to raise skepticism. According to Arthur C. Clarke, "Every revolutionary idea seems to evoke three stages of reaction. (1) It's completely impossible. (2) It's possible, but it's not worth doing. (3) I said it was a good idea all along."

I hope my journey inspires you to step up and do what you came here to do. A vast jigsaw puzzle of a different reality is unfolding, and we each have a unique piece. Together, we can create the tapestry of a new reality with the highest good for everyone.

We live in strange, exciting times, witnessing the old paradigm's chaotic death while birthing a new reality.

I invite you to read on and discover astonishing secrets.

With love and gratitude,
    Dr. Cynthia Miller

BOOK 1

COSMIC SECRETS

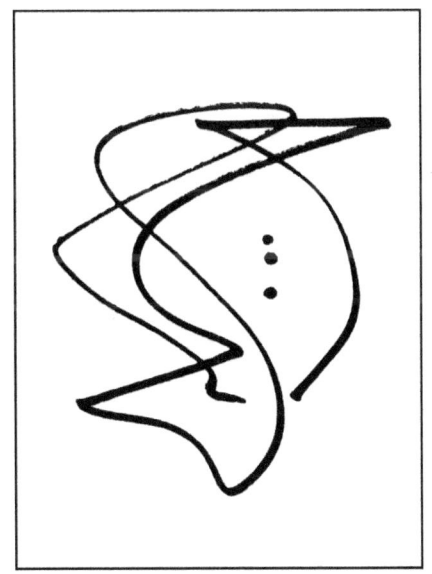

VW SPACE ODYSSEY
1989

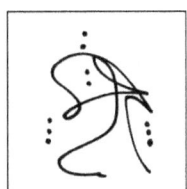

Worn windshield wipers flap, my bald tires skid on black ice. A strip of wiper-blade rubber snakes across the windshield, whipping over built-up frost—the defroster hums. Snow flurries melt on the window.

The flat plateau between Santa Fe and Taos, New Mexico, is sliced in two by the winding Rio Grande. The setting sun's long rays illuminate the red and purple cliffs on the other side of the gorge; magnificent colors glint beneath clumps of snow.

Around the bend, the road plummets to the bottom of the canyon. Slowly pumping my brakes, descending the plateau, my car swerves. Five-foot banks of snow line the narrow road, leaving no escape route. The wipers swish, clearing a patch to peer through.

At the bottom of the ravine, two cars collided, each sideways on a narrow bridge, leaving no path for my car to squeeze through. Four people stand at the edge of the bridge.

I'm terrified. I envision my car crashing on the bridge. Broken glass, shattered bones, ripped flesh, blood. I don't want to think about the possible gory details. Instead, I flip my consciousness and concentrate on the angels.

I flash back to when I was a small child, and I flew with the angels every night. On my first solo mission, I was allowed to swoop in and pull on the emergency brake to stop an unattended runaway car careening downhill.

A leap of consciousness is required, beyond the known, into the extraordinary. The angels are my only hope. I've been working with a team of angels with my clients for decades, and miraculous results occur. I need a miracle. I focus on the angels with all my might. If I lose concentration, if my mind tumbles into fear, I'll be rubble on the bridge.

There is no way I can maneuver through the crashed cars, let alone have enough momentum to make it up the hill. Heart pounding, mind racing, loudly chanting, "Angels help me, angels help me." I fixate on the angelic realms. Slow, long, deep breaths calm my racing heart. I release my tight grip on the wheel. Fingers lightly touch the cold slate grey steering wheel, one foot on the gas, the other on the brake, both doing nothing.

The only way is to surrender. I close my eyes. I know if I peek, my left brain will tumble into fear. One slip of consciousness, one doubt, one trace of fear, and I'm a mashed-up pile of broken glass, mangled metal, and crushed body. My eyes shut, beckoning the angels; I feel the car going downhill.

Suspended, I'm soaring through time and space. Was it a split second or longer? Who knows? Floating through space, my red VW and I are transported from one canyon wall across the river to the other canyon wall.

An unseen pressure on my right foot accelerates the car, and I feel it going uphill. My eyes now open, and I discover I'm past the bridge, about a third of the way up the hill, on the opposite side of the river. Gazing in the rearview mirror reveals astonished faces. I want to know what happened, but if I stop, the car will slide down, joining the others crushed on the bridge.

The whole way home, I replayed the scenario in my head, searching for a way to wrap my left brain around the incident. My linear thinking couldn't reconcile what had occurred; it was beyond 3-D perception. Trust, an open heart, and a multi-dimensional angelic connection provided my path to safety. When I surrender to my inner wisdom rather than my left-brain thinking, miraculous events occur.

After the incident, I wondered what transpired when I flew through space in my VW. From my current perspective, my car flew on angel wings, soaring from one side of the canyon, above the bridge and the river, to the other side—an initiation into the ninth dimension and angelic realms.

It's now time to make the quantum leap into another reality, one based on love, justice, and equality for all. The path is through the unknown, hidden deep within.

But first, it's crucial to grasp the underpinnings of this life.

HIDING IN PLAIN SIGHT
1948

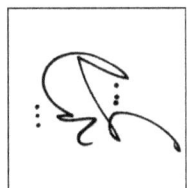

A cold, wet, smelly tongue licks my hand. Unknown dogs wander through the stark master bedroom at the back of the house where my parents, sister, and I sleep. The bars of my crib keep the dogs out but also leave me feeling helpless and trapped. A cloud of fear washes over me; there is no safety, no protection. It's 1948; I'm two.

When I fell asleep again, the angels whisked me away from the trepidation of the night. My first memories of the angels are those nights with the dogs and the confines of my crib. I soar with mighty wings that curve upward, expand out, taper toward the bottom, and cascade into two points. Spiraling, effortless, gliding through space, I love my nightly angelic flights.

We live in a house shell with bare cement floors, grey cement block walls, and a roof. Piles of rubble, dirt, and scattered bits of lumber fill the front yard. There's no front door. Pipes for the sink and the washing machine poke out into an empty kitchen. Dusty animal tracks on the floor lead out the unfinished kitchen doorway to the dirt backyard. The bathroom has a toilet and a sink, but no shower. The lime-acid smell of out-gassing unpainted cement burns my nose. Wind flutters through the missing door to the backyard and wisps of redwood pine needles scurry across the floor.

The photo was taken in the living room, with the kitchen to the left and the master bedroom in the background.

Dad designed the house around four stately redwood trees and gave the contractor the blueprints and a massive chunk of change. Dad's so enthralled with his job that he doesn't bother to check on our house. On the day we moved in, much to my parents' horror, we discovered the contractor had taken the money and skipped town.

Over time, windows appear, doors are installed, and the bathroom and kitchen become completed. A long narrow kitchen table attached to the wall folds up and down and is propped up with a wooden bar. Nasty prickly cactus fills the front yard flower beds. I move into my own room.

The Cold War between Russia and the United States is escalating. Radio broadcasts spread fear that Russia is gaining power. According to the news, the Commies loom large, ready to devour America's dearly held values of peace, democracy, and freedom. On January 30, 1950, President Truman responded—he ordered the clandestine construction of the H-bomb, unbeknownst to Russia and the American public.

Dad is the head construction engineer, surreptitiously building the world's first hydrogen bomb in the South Pacific. The arms race ignited. American hidden war tactics dominate. Who can make the deadliest weapon the fastest? Who can destroy more lives the quickest? Who can terrorize the world the most?

Photo before Dad leaves to create the world's first H-bomb.

The routine starts when Dad is gone for thirteen months building the H-bomb. I'm four, in kindergarten; Mom ships me off to school a year early to get me out of the house. To cope with the loneliness and fear-driven bomb dropping, Mom establishes her evening ritual. Every night, she slides into bed with a cheap bottle of red wine, a Hershey's chocolate bar, and a trashy Harlequin romance novel from the five-and-dime lending library a few blocks away. Every morning, I bring her coffee in bed.

Heavy, squeaky, wood kitchen drawers, pulled partway out, become my stairs. I climb up to the green with white speckles Formica countertop with a large silver metal edge. The countertop is cold on my feet; I reach up, open the cupboard, and get everything I need to make breakfast and my school lunch. A peanut butter and jelly sandwich on thin white bread; I had the same lunch every school day for nine years.

I make myself a bowl of sugar-frosted flakes with heaps of extra sugar on top, all drenched in milk for breakfast. Two or three mornings a week, every week for years, sitting on a barstool at the foldout kitchen table, I pass out. Head swirling, a black void appears, and my torso slumps against the edge of the counter. My feet fly up, knocking the wooden bar that holds up the kitchen breakfast bar; I slide head-first into the cement floor. My head bashed into the floor thousands of times, pounds in my feeling worthless, unlovable, and uncared for.

Lying helpless amidst broken glass, mounds of sugar, and soggy cereal, alone, Mom sips her coffee and screams from her bed, "Why didn't you eat sooner?"

Unbreakable melamine plastic dishes replace broken bowls. The rebuilt kitchen table doesn't collapse anymore. No one bothered or considered to check if something needed fixing in me.

I love my nightly flying with the angels in a magical world entered through the right hemisphere of my brain. My wings soar as I fly with grace in the middle of the group. The head angel is in the lead, directing our journey to the dimension of the healing angels. Luscious colors of light, form, and music surround me—a transparent, luminous holographic universe. The radiance makes life on Earth look flat and dull.

We make frequent visits to celestial healing centers. Four pillars of luminescent light mark the space. Inside a table or platform floats in mid-air, surrounded by the healing angels, a group of glowing beings that work together as a team to help humans in need. I'm resting on the table, concentrated beams of light shine, clearing nuclear radiation from my body. My visits to the healing temples with the angels keep me alive. Sweet music fills the air, and the aroma of heavenly flowers wafts as the angels perform healing miracles. The angels and I became great friends.

One morning, I happily announced, "Mom, I flew with the angels last night."

"Don't you ever talk about angels again." The fear of death oozed from her quivering voice. Nuclear warfare is conceived in our house; angels are not welcome. Anything out of line is suspicious. Flying with angels is unacceptable. I develop my secret world with the angels. Since I kept quiet, my nightly adventures are safe, beyond the ridicule and negative judgment of my mother.

It's a relief to go to sleep, escape the pain in my body, and be with the angels. At home, there was no show of love or affection. No hugs or kisses. No reading bedtime stories to the kids. No getting tucked in at night. I felt so crappy, I always put myself to bed; I wanted to escape the earth and fly with the angels.

One night, we are on a mission, flying low above the planet. My wings float through space with joyful freedom and ease. Flying near the Earth, we come to a city with steep hills. An empty car is slowly rolling downhill. Since no one is around, I'm allowed to do this mission alone. I fly into the vehicle and pull on the handbrake as hard as possible. The car screeches to a halt. There is a grand celebration of my success.

I wake up excited. I want to tell Mom about my escapade, and then realize I'm not allowed to talk about angels. When I open my eyes, cold gray cement walls and floors surround me. A lifeless house filled with fear and secrets. Not a spark of love to be found anywhere. Every morning, I land in a linear left-brain world filled with violence.

We live on Calaveras Street, which in Spanish means skull; our house is built from the ground up on deception, lies, and stealing. The structure, like a bunker, reflects the lies we propagate. The atmosphere comprises bombs, terror, and power-grabbing. We have no choice but to keep quiet and put up a fake front.

Inside the tight structure of the cement blocks, a need for secrecy rules. Our residence hides us in plain sight, a cement bunker war zone, smack dab in the middle of the suburbs. My Dad is one of three or four men on Earth who knows how to take the chalkboard scratching of the world's most advanced quantum physicist's equations and transform that into the physical construction of the world's first hydrogen bomb.

When a bomb explodes, there is a massive burst of light followed by waves of enormous destruction. My father's delight was to build bigger bombs with greater spheres of devastation. The living room coffee table was filled with top-secret documents and maps with circles around the target, showing how far the destruction spread. Since it was just my mother, my sister, and I, and we were women, we were seen as stupid, inferior, and worthless, so it was fine to leave the top-secret documents around the house.

I know my Dad worked for the Atomic Energy Commission and built bombs, but that's about all I know logically. Energetically, I pick up everything. Like a sponge, my tiny body absorbs the frequencies of bombs, hatred, and destruction. Repeated exposure to nuclear radiation weaves into my nervous system, held in my DNA, bones, and organs.

I don't understand why it's so nasty on Earth during the day and so luscious at night when I'm with the angels. My body hurts, and people aren't loving; the difference between day and night becomes excruciating.

"Mom, I have a headache," I called from my room.

Lying in bed, drinking her coffee, she calls back, "Take a pill."

The hall linen closet reeks of a hospital's gagging aroma with an undercurrent of the toxic smell of man-made chemicals. I stick my head in to reach the back of the shelf and rummage through the jumble of boxes and bottles of bitter-tasting pills and foul-flavored syrups. "Should I take the red ones or the white ones?"

"I don't care, take whatever you think," Mom calls back.

I live in two realities, on two dimensions, the 3-D and the angelic realms. During the day, I exist in the linear, logical left brain, the fear-conditioning amygdala, and the ancient reptilian brain that takes over when triggered by panic. Terror runs deep. My fear-based left brain develops.

The right side of my brain is also forming, the part connected to the infinite, angels, and my inner seeing. The right brain is expansive, loving, encompassing, and connected. My lucid dreaming is as vivid and bright as my waking state. Side-by-side, two different realities exist, each one growing in a contrasting part of my brain.

According to developmental biologist Dr. Bruce Lipton, in *The Biology of Belief,* our brains function in a delta state during the first six or seven years of life, a hypnogogic trance state with no discrimination.

Our inherited and childhood circuitry influences every aspect of our lives. Everything we learn in early childhood is absorbed and becomes the fundamental truth wired in our neural programming. About 95% of our thoughts, behaviors, and emotional responses originate from subconscious programs we imprinted from other people when we were children. The first seven years of life are also the time we learn self-identity.

Dad builds bombs; I fly with angels; I'm quiet about both.

WHY DO PEOPLE KILL EACH OTHER?
1951

Four cots line the walls, each with a pillow, sheets, and blankets. Rows of canned goods interspersed with giant bottles of water are stacked high on the wooden shelves braced against the far wall, storing enough food for four people to last about a week. A small rectangular table with four chairs holds a radio, a wind-up clock, a stack of candles, a box of matches, a 1st aid kit, flashlights, and a few books. The bomb shelter is ready.

It's 1951, and fear and panic of nuclear attack increase as news about the Cold War spreads. My good friend Jackie lives around the corner on Sinaloa Avenue. Sometimes we sneak down the cold cement stairs to play in the dark, dismal fortress of her family's basement bomb shelter.

When found, Jackie's mom hurries us out of the hideout. Walking up the steps from the gloomy basement into the light, I see a vision of an exploding bomb. A fiery mushroom cloud rises from the Earth, billowing and blocking out the sky. The Earth rumbles, and shock waves travel across the land. I see a clear image of wind blowing the cloud of grey smoke through the neighborhood, and everyone hiding inside for a few days. Then they will come out believing that everything will be OK. I don't understand how adults don't see the long-range implications of nuclear warfare and radiation.

A few weeks later, after watching the world's first hydrogen bombs explode, Dad returns home from the South Pacific. Gone for thirteen months, he brings exotic gifts I've never seen before: coconut, fresh pineapple, plumeria and gardenia leis, and grass hula skirts.

Photo US Air Force

It's painful to sit still at dinner. My father's looming presence dictates a no-nonsense attitude. Wiggling around is not acceptable. The hard wooden chairs are uncomfortable. I squirm, shaking my pigtails, stabbing my fork at my bland, dried-up fried hamburger patty. Hiding my frozen peas under the minute mashed potatoes, I see another vision of an exploding bomb. Energetically, I pick up everything from my Dad. Even though my five-year-old mind can't understand the implications of what I'm seeing, the image is distinct. I can't figure out how to separate the radiation from the water, soil, and the inside of the plants.

I pipe up, "Who will clean up the mess?" In my innocence, I asked Dad how to remove the radiation from the water and plants. A heavy silence fills the room. He slides back his chair, stands up, points his finger at me, and sends me to my room for the only time ever.

Hugging my knees, scrunched in the tight space in the corner between the wall and my bird's-eye maple dresser, I feel alone, frightened, and know I should keep quiet. I can't figure out why adults are so stupid and don't fathom the mess they are creating.

That night triggers the trajectory of my life; an internal spark ignites while I hide in the corner, feeling scared, powerless, and worthless. Even though I'm just a girl of no value, I want to stop the fear and violence.

The imprint of exploding bombs awakens my awareness of the astonishing depth of hatred, torture, and cruelty people inflict upon each other. At the time, I didn't understand humanity's collective unconscious filled with fear, horror, and torment that perpetuates war and violence.

That night, my lifelong search to discover my worth and why people kill each other switched on. My life is a windy path through bliss and torture as the outer violence turns inward. The external brutality of the world is wired into the cellular structures of my body.

I keep quiet. I hide my brilliance, even from myself.

TRAIN HOPPING IN IRAN
1959

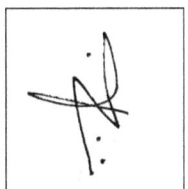

The Cold War is coming to a close; there is a moratorium on nuclear testing. Instead of building and dropping bombs, Dad's now the project manager of a sugar cane plantation and refinery in the isolated desert of Iran. I haven't seen him in ten months. After a whirlwind tour of Europe, Mom, my sister, and I met up with Dad in Teheran.

The next day we board the train for an eighteen-hour trip into the remote vastness of Iran. Women carrying water and heavy baskets on their heads and caravans of camels dot the countryside. The train passes by towns with shimmering azure tiled mosques, towering minarets, and bustling bazaars. Women camouflaged in black are indistinguishable. It's 1959, and the women are not entirely concealed in a burqa, women wear chadors, long black robes that cover their head and body, leaving their faces uncovered. Hidden from man's voracious gaze, the woman must remain unseen.

En route to Southern Iran, the train jolts to a stop at one of the many villages. A girl appearing my age approaches the train. She stands next to the tracks, one foot away from our compartment window, the glass insulating my world from hers. My body sinks into the plush maroon velvet seat as she reaches her hand out begging—a barefoot girl in dirty rags, a naked baby on each hip. Flies crawl in their eyes; snot drips from their noses as their tiny smiles broaden.

For the first time, I grasp my privileged life. It never occurred to me that everyone wasn't similar to me. All my friends at school and the kids in the neighborhood came from relatively similar economic backgrounds. I knew some people were a lot richer, but I had never seen this depth of poverty.

The girl in rags and I locked eyes; we searched deep into each other's souls. An internal dichotomy arises in my guts. On the inside, I feel unlovable and worthless, and yet I'm sitting on an elegant velvet cushion in a 1st class train compartment lined with polished mahogany with brass fittings—a waterfall of emotions cascades through my body. I feel guilt and shame about my privilege. If I was born in a different situation, I could be that girl begging, holding a naked baby on my hips. She was born in poverty in Iran; I was born in Southern California. My birth granted me entire worlds unavailable to this girl. Who am I to be given this privilege?

At the same time, an inner knowing emerges, in our essence, we are similar; we're both humans living on this earth, there's no difference between us. We are both impoverished, me internally, she externally, each a victim of circumstance. Gazing in her eyes, a worthless feeling washes over my body. And then the terrifying insight arises; we are both worthless because we are female.

The train pulls out of the station, heading further south into the interior of Iran. After seventeen and a half hours, as the dawn is breaking, Dad hunts for the man with the keys to open the passenger doors.

Poking my head out of the window, I see spirals of smoke billowing near the railroad track. There is no train stop; some of the Americans built a fire by the side of the tracks to alert the conductor. Squeaking brakes slow down the train. Twelve bright yellow, blue, and pink paisley print suitcases fly off the moving train, landing on the sun-baked desert. We jump off. We're home.

I'm tired and stunned. The sight is shocking. Haft Tapeh, or Seven Hills, is the village where we live. Not a shantytown of the edge of a

Cosmic Inner Seeing

city, this village is plopped down in the middle of nowhere. To the left of the train tracks are mud huts, no doors, no plumbing or electricity, virtually unchanged for thousands of years. Through the center of the dirt street runs the gutter or jube. The waterway, women squat washing and getting drinking water, animals wander through, and kids play, all in the same dirty, smelly, infected water. The stench is horrible.

To the right of the tracks sits our settlement. Tall white foreigners construct huge houses up on top of the nearest hill. Dad's been here for ten months, overseeing the building of the project from the ground up. Strange things like running water, flushing toilets, and glass windows appear. Typewriters, swivel office chairs, and refrigerators arrive, things never imagined or seen before by the villagers. At night, lights beam on the hill like an alien space station.

The mail and a kilo of pale green salted pistachios arrive every two weeks. Newspapers from Teheran give us a glimpse into Iranian culture. One headline read, "Daughter claims father has wed thirty-six times." According to Muslim culture, a man can have four permanent wives and as many temporary wives as he wants.

We search through the mail, awaiting news from home, study the latest *Vogue* and read the Sunday funnies, all while cracking open the most delicious pale green pistachios. Mom's one prerequisite for living in the middle of nowhere is her subscription to *Vogue* magazine.

There are no phones, and no way to communicate except by mail, every two weeks. Today I received a letter from my new friend, Susan. On our way to Iran, we took a cruise from New York to Southampton, England. Standing on the deck, cheering, waving goodbye to unknown faces in the crowd below, the boat pulls away from New York harbor. Confetti floats through the air.

Mom turns to the woman standing next to her, who has two kids, a young son, and a daughter about my age, and asks if they are on vacation. The woman replies that they are on their way to join her husband in Iran. Our jaws drop. None of Mom's friends have heard of Iran, much less knows where it is. Here, standing next to us, the first people we speak to on a crowded ocean liner are a woman with two kids headed for Iran.

Mom replies that we are also on our way to Iran to Haft Tapeh, where Dad is building a sugar cane plantation and refinery for the Shah. Introductions made. We learn that Betty Engle and her daughter Susan and son Tom will be living at the Army base in Ahwaz.

We stare in amazement at each other. The Statue of Liberty shrinks into the horizon. Susan, who is one year older than me, and I hang out together on the ship, going to the movies, playing in the pool, and sitting in the Adirondack deck chairs checking out the boys. We become great friends.

Now settled in Ahwaz, Susan invites me down for a two-week visit. I am excited to see someone my age, so I quickly write back to confirm the dates.

The southbound train comes through at the first light of dawn. It takes a team of people to catch the train in Haft Tapeh. A fire needs to be built to alert the conductor. When the train slows down, people start banging on the doors and windows to alert the guy with the key to open the door. Sometimes the wrong people get pulled in through the windows, and they have to jump off again.

Through all the craziness, somehow my suitcases and I are on the train. Safely on board, through the open door, I watch a group of half-naked barefoot children run after camels. They pick up the fresh, warm camel dung and slap the muck into patties, larger and thinner than a hamburger, and line the patties in the sun to dry. The dried camel dung is used for fuel to cook food and heat water.

Afraid to be in one of the compartments with only men, I sit at a table in the dining car. I know how to read numbers in Farsi, and my few Persian words are enough to order tea, and pay the bill. I order chai, which is strong black tea in Iran.

Slurp, gurgle, slosh, the men next to me are drinking their tea Iranian style, with a lump of sugar held between their teeth, sipped from a glass. The man sitting across from me has no front teeth from this sugar habit. Bushy eyebrows partially hide his piercing, menacingly dark eyes. Black cotton chadors camouflage women on the streets, and the bare arms of a young western girl are a rare sight, especially alone on a train.

Ahwaz is a large town with an official train station and stop. As the train slows down, I break out in a sweat. Will Susan be there to meet me? I have no idea where she lives or how I could get there. No taxis, no telephones, no hotels, all the signs in Farsi, out the train window I see an expanse of beggars. I'm thirteen; it's 1959.

I'm almost dizzy getting off the train. My head pokes out the top of the crowd, my blond hair, blue eyes, and light skin, a sight most have never seen before. The reek of feces, urine, and rotting garbage is enough to gag a maggot.

I'm greeted by a suffocating swarm of little boys in dirty rags clambering around me, begging for money. Cut off limbs, twisted, deformed bodies. They pull on my clothes and jam their grubby little hands in my face, all screaming *baksheesh*, which means give me money. Disease carrying flies crawl in their eyes. At my feet, deformed beggars vie for my attention.

In the begging class, the parents deliberately break bones, cut off limbs, and deform their babies, so they grow up to be better beggars. My stomach turns at the violence people do to each other. The experience is harrowing. Terror hits me. What if Susan doesn't show up?

I squirm my way through the crowd carrying my matching pink paisley train case and suitcase. A pack of children follows me, yelling, "*Baksheesh*." I finally reach the area with the cars, and there is Susan with her driver. We give each other a big hug—waves of relief wash over my body.

As the driver is weaving through crowded streets, Susan and I are so excited to see each other. We catch up on what has happened since our last visit. Driving through the bazaar in Ahwaz is a stark contrast to sitting on the ship's teak deck chairs overlooking the pool and the expanse of the ocean. We pull up to Susan's house in the military compound.

What I remember most about my visit is how strange the Army Base felt, and why it was there. It was wonderful to be with Susan, but the air was filled with American dominance, authority, and superiority.

Two weeks later, on the ride home, I'm the only one in the dining car. In a contemplative daze, I gaze out the window—sandy blasts of heat ripple across the endless vista of cracked, dried earth. The hot sun bakes the desert into six-inch to eight-inch jagged pieces that are about one inch thick. The cracks in the earth resemble the fractures forming in my belief system.

The Iranian culture is so different from the American view of life. Before I lived in Iran, it never occurred to me that there was another way to view reality. I assumed that my way was the only way, the correct way. I began to speculate, who is right?

People assume their culture and religion is the right way. Beyond lifestyle and belief, we all are people and want the same things -- food and shelter, our families, friends, happiness, love, and safety. I wonder if it's possible to have a different reality where women are valued, and people don't hate and kill each other. The setting sun jars me out of my contemplation.

The northbound train leaves Ahwaz late in the afternoon, and it is dark by the time it reaches Haft Tapeh. With no electricity, it is impossible to spot in the dark of night.

I search for a man with keys to unlock the train door. Will anyone remember I'm coming home tonight? Is anyone at the railroad tracks building a fire? The screech of the train wheels signals the train is slowing down. The door unlocked, I threw my bags out the train door and jumped off the moving train.

Cosmic Inner Seeing

Every so often, a Mercedes pulls up in front of our house; it is one of the sheikhs from the nearby village of Susa bearing gifts to buy off my Dad. The most exquisite fine silk and Persian wool carpets grace the floor as offerings. The sheikhs, rulers of the tribe or village, love to '*baksheesh*' or bribe my Dad into hiring more workers from their communities since they get a cut of each of their villager's wages.

According to Iranian custom, if Dad accepts the gifts, at a later time, the sheikh can demand me in return. This practice leaves me feeling vulnerable and nervous since, at thirteen, I'm prime marrying age. My sister is seventeen, too old to be married off. I am the chief's daughter, blonde hair, blue-eyed, a rare, delicious morsel to become one of the sheikh's many wives.

Being traded for a rug ripples through my bones, igniting deep terror. I don't know if I have any worth. I drop into the collective fear of being worthless scum; that my only value is to serve male authority, with little or nothing in return. The land, culture, and collective consciousness carry these low-frequencies, like the hot sun surging over the dry, barren desert. I am a second-rate, inferior, girl, with little, or no significance.

Hiding in the back of the closet, I can't comprehend if I have any worth. I don't know if a Persian carpet is more important than me. Am I to be exchanged for a rug to cater to the sheikh's bidding? To become one of his multiple wives to indulge his sexual pleasures, to cook, clean, and take care of him in exchange for scraps of food and shelter.

There's no inner safety in knowing that I'm cherished and valued. The only inner knowing I have is, if I disagree, I'll be bombed.

During the construction of the sugar cane refinery, a road cut through a mound of earth. The exposed straight vertical fissure reveals an ancient burial ground. Evidence of an opulent culture lies at our feet as we meander in and out of the crumbling brown earthen rubble. The sweltering desert sands whistle horizontally across the barren desert. The blowing sands, composed of sharp tiny rocks, smash into my arms, legs, and face. I'm standing on the land of the Persian King Darius the Great, where 2,500 years ago, the empire's breadbasket was lush and verdant. It's now a wasteland, alternately parched and flooded, where summer temperatures reach 118 degrees.

Next to substantial intact clay burial urns, we find small clay pots full of coins. Bronze irregular coins, the head of a man on one side, the other side little ridges or bumps. Bits of pottery, and the occasional piece of broken shimmering, opalescent purple-turquoise thin glass bracelet, are evidence of this magnificent civilization.

I discover pieces of a small female clay figure. Every woman had a little female statue. When she died, it was broken into three sections, the head and legs broken off from the torso. Clay vessels with rounded bottoms used for oil were in perfect condition. We found a piece of cuneiform writing on an Elamite tablet dating back to 3,500 BCE.

A rich, lush culture crumbled beneath our feet. This era of affluence declined into poverty at the deepest level of basic survival. Now, a rudimentary culture exists; illiteracy prevails.

Horse hooves thunder, the earth trembles; men on Arabian horses suddenly charge towards me. Raised banners fly, turbans billow, long coats flow, and an expanse of movement spreads over the hills. The Arabians gallop with skillful momentum, dignity, and grace. It feels like a scene from Lawrence of Arabia, but this is not a movie.

My heart pounds, waving my arms in fright, I race past the men squatting in the dirt, hoping to get work for the day, to the office.

Cosmic Inner Seeing

"Look," I gasp, trying to catch my breath, "Look at all the men on horses."

"Yes," Dad replies, "Remember, the Shah of Iran is coming to visit today."

I'm wearing my best pink cotton party dress, short sleeves, knee-length skirt, in preparation for the Shah's visit. The importance of his arrival hadn't registered until seeing the men on horseback cresting the top of the slope.

Back at our house, chairs lined in straight rows in the front yard overlook the scene. Only Americans live on the hill; they gather, taking seats, waiting for the arrival of the special train carrying the Shah and his wife, Farah Pahlavi. Since Farah Pahlavi is pregnant with the potential future heir to the throne, she will remain on the train.

Off in the distance, more Arabian horses, flags, and men glide toward the railroad tracks. The horses and men stand in lines along the tracks, with no food or water, and wait patiently in the blazing sun for the Shah's arrival. Everyone is in their best clothes, baggy suits, or long robes cinched at the waist over many layers of clothes, with the traditional headdress, a loosely wrapped cotton fabric.

A loud noise appears out of nowhere, an unknown sight to most of these men, the Shah's helicopter arrives and lands next to the railroad tracks.

Mac, one of the Americans, calls out, "Cynthia, would you like a ride in the Shah's helicopter?"

"YES," I reply.

Mac hops in the front of the open jeep, and I jump in back. We drive down the hill, past the line of horses and men. These men have never seen someone with eyes the color of azure mosque tiles and pale bare arms and legs emerging from a pink dress. Their eyes penetrate through me as the jeep bounces towards the helicopter. I'm the only female present among hundreds of men. Through my father, I have privilege and status, not because of my own worth.

We fly low over the village revealing women hiding behind walls, trying to peek out. Iranian women are not allowed at events of this nature. Small bunches of women and children clutched together, looking up at us soaring in the sky, awe, wonder, and shock fills their faces.

The canal, originally built by Darius the Great, 2,500 years ago, feeds water to the sugar cane fields. The temperature cools as we glide over numerous varieties of sugarcane undulating in waves from the movement of the propellers. As the helicopter flies over the sugar refinery and adjacent buildings, off in the distance, the speck of a moving train catches our eyes. The helicopter circles back over the mud huts of the village, the railroad tracks lined with men on their horses, and the western houses built up on the hill, overlooking all.

The village is the same as it has been for millennia, yet up on the hill, the houses have hot and cold running water, long comfy couches, record players, and stacks of classical, jazz, and Elvis Presley records.

When the train arrives, the Shah greets the men. Presented with three animal offerings, at first, the Shah refuses the gifts but then agrees to sacrifice only the lamb.

I witnessed the extinction of a lifestyle known for thousands of years and the beginning of a new era. Today, Haft Tapeh is a booming city. Photos on Google Maps show houses with doors and windows, and electrical wires dangling along paved tree-lined streets. Videos of the Khuzestan sugar cane refinery workers are on YouTube.

Iran's collective consciousness of women's lack of value strikes a deep resonance. How do I find my worth in a world that treats women as second-rate?

SWISS BOARDING SCHOOL
1960

In the spring, I'm off to the magic of Switzerland to school. Alone, I fly from Abadan in Southern Iran, change planes in Rome, and land in Zürich. One of the teachers meets me, and we travel by train to Neuchâtel, to the northern tip of Lake Geneva. I'm fourteen; it's 1960.

Silent on the train, I absorb lush Swiss protection. Snowcapped Alps soar, soft green rolling hills undulate, in stark contrast to the hard-baked Iranian desert. Craggy snow-covered peaks tumble down into waves of green grass. The crisp, clean, fresh air revives my senses. Sheltered in the beauty and grace of the Swiss Alps, I feel safe.

I've always loved the mountains. When I was a kid, we went camping in Yosemite, Sequoia, and Kings Canyon, times of joy and delight, being nourished by nature. Sparkling lakes, steep winding mountain roads, big trees, I'm in my element.

Confused, exhausted, and disoriented, I fall asleep in a room with six beds. In the night, three Spanish-speaking girls pull the pillow out from under my head and unroll a huge feather duvet. They stick the pillow back under my head and fluff the duvet over me, all while giggling. I wake up in an empty room, get dressed, and wait.

A maid finds me and speaks Italian. When she figures out I'm an American, she grabs my hand and pulls me upstairs. She swings open a door, and one of the girls calls out, "Are you an American?" I'm relieved to find someone who speaks English, who can tell me where to get breakfast.

The crème de la crème, La Chatelainie, is a Swiss finishing school for daughters from influential families around the world, heads of state, powerful business tycoons, brilliant minds, and Hollywood movie stars. Most have fathers of power; on some level, many of us are treated the same, like a pretty little appendage that acts politely and knows when to be quiet and when to leave. At the time, it never occurred to me that my father was also a man of power.

The isolation of Iran soon dissolves; I'm sharing a room with girls from all over the world. At first, I felt like I didn't belong; eventually, these girls became the first real family I've ever known. I don't have to explain myself. I can be who I want to be. Relieved from revolving around my parents, I'm now fed fresh, healthy food, laughing with my friends, and a whole new world opens.

I can take a breath and not worry about being killed, annihilated, or shredded to bits by exploding bombs. I test my limits. I push the school rules to see how far I can go. I know when I'm back in the States, I'll live in the cement-block bunker, even though the bombs have already exploded, radiation still exudes from the walls.

The school has two locations, St. Blaise, a small village outside of Neuchâtel, where I spend spring and autumn, and Gstaad, a renowned ski resort in the Swiss Alps, where I ski in the winter and enjoy the summer.

In St. Blaise, every morning on the way to school, I walk by the bakery with fresh croissants, pastries, and still-warm baguettes. The smell of fresh-baked bread drifts through the street. Piles of red and green grapes spill from wooden boxes in front of the fruit and vegetable shop. Bright red tomatoes glisten in the sun; a whiff of fresh mint fills the air. Further up the street, on the right side, is the butcher shop. Every Tuesday, someone carries a plate of beef brains from the slaughterhouse across the road to the butcher shop. Thursday mornings, it's cow tongue. The rest of the week, blood-red meat is carried across the lane on large metal trays.

Cosmic Inner Seeing

Around the corner from the school, half a block down on the right, vast open meadows filled with cows. An old stone building sits on the left. Inside, it's dark and cool, delicious cheese and yummy homemade yogurt with fresh fruit are for sale.

We study French six days a week. One day, I'm slithering out French words, and Madame Roulet, the beginning French teacher, is harassing my knuckles with her ruler. I pass out, slide out of my chair, and collapse into a lump on the floor. Madame Roulet freaks out, and from then on is pleasant to me. Her delight was to torment her students into learning. The girls who wore glasses had water flicked in their faces, so everything was a blurry mess. Around this time, a new level of headaches starts to occur.

One of my amusements is to sneak to town on the bus, walk around, and then come back. On one of my ventures, I get on the bus, and there is a teacher. I sit down next to her and start up a conversation. Madame Roulet is waiting at the bus stop in Saint Blaise, ready to snatch up wayward girls. When she saw me step off the bus with the teacher, she didn't bother to check the school records. It felt great to slip by the rules.

We become each other's family. Each of us is alone in a foreign country, away from everything we know, living in a strange place, speaking a language we don't fully understand. We bond on a profound level. We have each other's backs. A level of safety emerged I hadn't known before. And from that level of security, we had fun. We laugh and play, something very new for me; it's safe to be me.

For fun, we tie five bed sheets together and hang the sheet-rope out the second-story window. A group of girls holds one end. I climb out the window barefoot, in my nightgown, curlers in my hair, shimmy down the sheets, and run to the vending machine by the bakery to buy a package of cigarettes.

One night, inching my way up the sheets, my foot kicks the front door. A resounding bang echoes through the three-story house. We pull the sheets up the window and dive into our beds before the headmistress envelopes the room with her stern presence. I'm hiding under the covers, heart pounding, trying not to giggle.

We smoke cigarettes, which is forbidden. I don't know that I enjoyed inhaling tobacco smoke, but I have so much fun with cigarettes. We play games. We wet the rim of a glass to keep a paper napkin in place. Rip the edge of the napkin off, so the top of the glass looks like a drum. Then we put a centime, or the equivalent of a penny, in the center of the napkin. Taking turns, we burn holes and watch the cigarette embers devour the napkin until the coin is held up with slender threads of fire-eaten paper. The girl who makes the coin drop has to do a forfeit.

At times, teachers roam the hallways sniffing for smoke. Usually, we have a few moments' notice; we can hear her footsteps. We stash our ashtrays under the closets, the door bursts open, and the teacher calls out, "Qui fume ici?" or "Who's smoking in here?" As soon as she leaves, we dive under the closet to retrieve our dying cigarettes. One time, the standup closet fell over; the doors almost broke off.

Gstaad is like living in a storybook fantasy. Summers in Gstaad are divine. After a rigorous morning of French lessons, we spend our afternoons at the Palace Hotel lounging by the pool, playing bridge, with our coiffed hair, full skirts, stockings, and cat eye sunglasses.

Two different clubs emerge, jokingly called the BBC and the FCC. The BBC is the big-busted club, while the FCC is the flat-chested club. I'm a member of the FCC, four of us, all flat as a board. We are painfully aware that women are judged by the size of our breasts. How smart we are is of little consequence; our bodies' curves are of the utmost importance.

One of the girls in the FCC, Margot, and I communicate telepathically every day. The other two girls in the FCC kept getting pissed that we didn't include them in our talks. The only problem is that Margot and my discussions aren't with words; they're energetic. We knew what the other was thinking and what we would do next.

In the afternoon, fat cows with huge hand-painted cowbells walk through the center of town, heading home for the night. The village is about two blocks long; on the right is the pastry shop with amazing desserts. Every day, I buy a dozen pastries to eat on my way home. Across from the pastry shop is Charlie's, the local hangout where we play the cigarette game. Sometimes the girl who loses has to run up and kiss one of the Swiss army guys sitting at the next table.

Past the town, I wander the narrow path through fields of green grass and wildflowers up to my chalet. Chalet Sunbeam, nestled in the hills, has a sharply slanted roof; rustic wood decks line each of the three floors, overlooking the town and the nearby ski resort.

After a day of skiing, we hike up the hill to school in our clunky, soggy leather ski boots, carrying heavy 6-foot-long skis. Sometimes we hop on the back of a wagon carrying hay and ride up the hill. Walking to my chalet in the evening, snow crunches under my boots, sparkles of fairy dust snowflakes float through the air, glistening in the streetlights. The shop windows emit warmth and love, safety envelopes my body.

Before I came home, my mom threw out every scrap of my childhood —the quilt my grandmother made, my toys and secret notes, my antique treadle sewing machine that I used to sew my clothes, all gone. My childhood was in the trash; that's how much I mattered to my parents.

Returning home after two years, the shallowness of Southern California culture is shocking; it embodies the self-reflection of a flea; the focus is on material consumption. Surfing, the Beach Boys are the rage; talk, clothes, and activities revolve around the latest craze. What I wore to school is more important than what I thought. I have trouble understanding Southern Californian English, surfer slang, and colloquialisms- woodies (a type of car with wood panels), bitchin, groovy, the Beach Boys, hang ten, are beyond my comprehension.

In a foreign country, everything is fresh and different. Senses perk up, searching for clues on how to function. The awareness learned from traveling shifts how I see reality. The known, taken for granted, is jarring with new sensitivity and perspective.

The USA is a young culture designed for consumerism. Ugly architecture built for short-term gain contrasts with European architecture crafted for beauty and function, constructed to last for centuries. Southern California culture reflects the consciousness of immediate gratification.

Kids cruise Colorado Boulevard in hot cars on Friday night, showing off. The rage is Bob's Big Boy Drive-in. On my first date, we ordered over a speaker attached to a pole near the car, and a carhop arrived on roller skates, twirling around the cars, with two trays stacked with food. My window has to be rolled down to the perfect height for the tray to fit. We eat in his dark green Porsche, showing off, food on a scuffed silver metal tray hangs out the car window, a double-decker hamburger drips ketchup and mayonnaise, Coke, and French fries dipped in tartar sauce, we stare out the window. It's very different from sitting face-to-face and having a conversation.

In high school, I squish everything down. I've lived in the scorching desert of Iran, where I escaped being traded for a rug to become one of the sheik's multiple wives. At thirteen, I jumped on moving trains that took me to an ancient city filled with beggars. I learned to ski in the Swiss Alps; my best friends are from around the world. At night, I dream in French. My French accent was laughed at; everyone speaks a slang language I don't understand.

When I went to college, my mind exploded. I had a boyfriend who loved to read. He brought me books and recommended what to read next. A magical world opened that I didn't know existed, exploring different thoughts and ways of seeing the world. By the time I was in college, I had lived in four countries: the US, Iran, Switzerland, and India. I was well-traveled, but a foreigner to the world of literature.

Only a few good friends know about my living abroad; I keep quiet with everyone else. I scrunch myself into a small box to be vaguely accepted.

TEMPLE CARVINGS AND LOCUST INVASIONS

1964

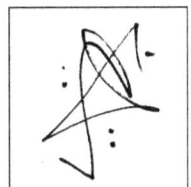

A rush of excitement surges through my body as I emerge from the airplane and step onto the shiny metal rolling staircase leading down to the cement tarmac.

I'm in San Francisco to visit my sister for a little getaway, hidden from our parents. Earlier that day, after school, I hopped in my car and drove to Los Angeles International Airport. I'm sixteen, living with a family in Altadena, CA., for my senior year of high school. Mom and Dad live in India.

My sister and I walked the long glass-lined corridor to the baggage claim and stopped to watch a plane from Hong Kong disembark. A tall man caught my eye. Much to our shock, walking down the steps of the aircraft is Dad; he has flown from India to San Francisco on a last-minute business trip. We meet him at the gate and exchange unforgettable moments of awe and wonder.

Even though we rarely see each other or communicate, there is an energetic connection, a tie linking us together.

One and a half years later, stepping off the airplane into the intense heat, the majestic Indian air, and a noisy, packed airport, I'm a bundle of mixed emotions. I'm always up for an adventure and an exciting trip; I'm hesitant about spending a hot summer in India with my parents. It's 1964; I'm eighteen.

I haven't seen Mom in about three years. A few days after arriving in India, she took me to one of her favorite places. Meandering through the narrow, crooked streets of the bazaar in Old Delhi, stepping through cow dung and pools of urine, snake charmers jam their snakes in my face, begging children tug on my clothes, while cockroaches crawl up my legs under my baggy Indian pants. The wrenching, filthy stench, swarming bugs, teeming people, and monsoon rains in the 117° heat make my skin crawl. It's the essence of hell.

Up the narrow, steep stairs, I behold a magnificent vision, a room full of silk. Every imaginable color was arranged like a rainbow, floor-to-ceiling bolts of silk. The walls were lined with everything from the softest charmeuse to delicate chiffon to heavy nubby raw silk. With a warp and weft of different colors, the shimmering of silk delights my senses, shades that almost resemble those of the angelic realms. I'm in heaven. Passed down in DNA, I inherited my mother's unique ability to see and differentiate a plethora of colors that most people don't detect.

The earthy smell of fabric mixed with the scent of natural dye permeates the room. My creativity ignited. How to choose which colors and what to sew? For decades after this trip, I dreamt of this room in India and the fabric.

About once a week, snake charmers grace the driveway of our house in New Delhi. A short man wearing a turban and off-white dhoti, or cloth around his waist and interlaced between his legs, arrives with a wooden flute and a dilapidated woven basket. He squats on the hot, bare cement driveway next to our dark green jeep, playing his flute. Slowly, the cobra weaves and bobs its head out of the old round basket. Meanwhile, the flute player's assistant is wrapping a ten-foot boa constrictor around his arms and neck. Deliberately, the cobra undulates, darting its head back and forth; it slithers out of the basket.

Eerie, off-key sounds float up to the second-story balcony; standing in utter horror, transfixed, I absorb the scene. I'm paralyzed in fear, terrified that the snakes will crawl up the stairs or the walls and capture me. Mom is sipping her scotch and eating peanuts, and Dad is nowhere to be found.

The heat, bugs, the power going on and off, the lack of good food, and Dad's traveling back and forth between Delhi, Khetri, and the USA all take their toll on Mom. Mom's way of coping with all of this is a fifth of scotch a day.

Inside the enormous metal gate, a circular drive opens to vistas of verdant grass and trees in stark contrast to the beggars in filthy rags, sitting in squalor, starving, outside the compound walls. Scottie, the owner of the estate, is Mom's black-market source for scotch.

His house, surrounded by a veranda on two sides, looks out over the refreshing green of the croquet lawn. Rattan chairs and chaise lounges with white linen cushions and hand-carved inlaid tables line the veranda. A tall, thin man dressed in a long, crisp white tunic shirt, tight-legged pants, and a white turban with a red feather stands erect, looking straight ahead, waiting for instructions. In a similar outfit with white-gloved hands, another man arrives with a round silver tray carrying tall glasses of iced tea and long, silver, carved iced tea spoons. It's 115 degrees, and ceiling fans slowly turn overhead, moving the hanging air gently throughout the veranda. It's arranged for me to have dinner with Scottie a few nights later.

Mom decides to repay Scottie or continue to get her scotch - I'm not sure which - I am to go out with him. I know my Mom and what might be at stake. The mark of a real alcoholic, Mom's booze connection is more precious than I am. I put on layers of clothes that cover me up and are challenging to undo. The heat is suffocating, but I'm wearing lots of layers. Once in the taxi, Scottie immediately starts groping me, pulling on my clothes, and kissing me. The Sikh taxi driver, wearing a grubby white turban and Sikh gentleman's beard net, keeps smiling, eyeing us in the rear-view mirror. I'm eighteen, and Scottie must be in his late forties. I protest, shouting no, and start demanding that the taxi driver take me home. The taxi driver pulls over, watches me fighting off Scottie, and smiles. There is no way the taxi driver will take me back at my request. During an insipid dinner, Scottie kept his hands off me; I arrived home intact.

At the time, I didn't have the inner capacity to confront my mother. My early childhood programming keeps me quiet, while my feelings of worthlessness render me silent. I have no authority over my mother, the taxi driver, or Scottie. I'm just a girl to be used for other people's pleasure or gain.

A week later, we rumbled over washboard dirt roads from New Delhi through remote regions in our sturdy jeep to Khetri, a small village in Rajasthan where Dad is building a copper mine.

Basic survival, starvation, and death permeate the air. A massive wave of famine spreads across India. In the morning, dead bodies line the gutter. I want to curl up in disgust and fear, or pretend it isn't happening. I have no inner mechanism to cope with this level of poverty; the shock of it all imprints in my unconscious. It's overwhelming and terrifying to witness survival, poverty, and famine at this rock bottom level.

We stop near a majestic white marble temple. The villagers have never seen anyone like me before. I am tall with blonde hair, blue eyes, eighteen, and a woman. Dirt swirls, kids swarm around me like a pack of flies, yank on my clothes, and try to stick their filthy fingers in my eyes.

My dusty feet touch freshly washed, cool marble. The stillness and silence in the temple feel familiar and welcoming—an ember of inner knowing kindles. Carvings of serpents twined together, hand gestures, and sacred geometry stir an inner knowing—a safe refuge from the filth, heat, and tiny germ-infested fingers creeping into my eyes.

Evidence of famine is everywhere. Proof of the temporary, delicate nature of the human body is exposed in India, and so well hidden in the States. I wonder how people survive; most of our food comes from the black market. In Iran, the crippled children begging were horrendous; in India, poverty and starvation are staggering. Unconscious festering spreads, inner guilt, and shame about my privilege, while so many others worldwide live in deprivation and cruel hardship.

Back on the road, the driver starts shouting, "OK, boss, OK, boss?" Sitting in the back seat of the jeep, I wonder what's happening. The driver swerves and hits a peacock. The driver jumps out, runs over and catches the bird, wrings its neck, and throws it in the back. He quickly jumps in and drives off before anyone sees him. The peacock thrashes around for a few moments and then lies limp on the floor, displaying its magnificent colors.

We arrive at two houses in the middle of a field, the assistant directors' and ours. We have tough peacock for dinner, and Mom has a new collection of iridescent purple and royal blue feathers.

In the bathroom corner, gooey green slime and mold cascade from the ceiling down into the tub. Cockroaches abound in the soggy, smelly, damp room. There are two choices for bathing that I'm aware of at the time. One is the shower. Chances are very high that once the shampoo is in my hair, the power will go off, and the water will stop. The water can be off for a few hours to a numerous days. With this option, there is the definite possibility of having soapy hair and body for days, which isn't fun in 120° weather. The other option is to take a bath and scoop the cockroaches onto the floor with a cup.

An inch gap exists between the outside door and the floor in my sister's and my bedroom. The thinking is that when the roof leaks during monsoon season, all the water can run out under the door. Many nights, we find snakes and scorpions that enter during the heat of the day. In the dark, tiny fluorescent green bugs randomly hitting one small lampshade sound like light rain. In the morning, green bug snot drips from my nose. I wonder how many I've eaten. Mosquito netting is not in Mom's consciousness. Fixing the bedroom door and the leaky roof isn't significant enough to be considered. Our safety is of no concern.

Creepy crawlies dart up my legs; the Khetri Copper mine is a blasted hole in the Earth. Walking up a hard dirt-packed ramp, emaciated men slowly emerge from the hot cave, barefoot, clad in rags, carrying baskets on their heads filled with rocks and bits of copper. The site makes my stomach turn, the inhumanity that feeds corporate greed.

It's finally time to return to Delhi. Driving down the crumbly road, we round a curve, and I see my first sadhu, or holy man. Covered in sacred ash, he stands naked, long matted dreadlocks, beady eyes, a tall trident in his right hand. Stained teeth, red betel nut juice drips from his lips.

Three white ashen streaks across his forehead, his eyes reveal an altered state I've never encountered before. I gaze in amazement with curiosity and wonder as Dad tries to divert my attention.

Down the road, I see a massive tree with large leaves. In shock, I realize the leaves are vultures. Further on, vultures rip at and devour the flesh of a dead woman. Burning Ghats line the river, flames consume dead bodies; a few platforms raised on stilts hold corpses for the vultures to eat. The stench of burning flesh is horrific.

An hour later, a caravan of scrawny camels, laden with small children and earthly possessions covered with tarps, blocks the road. We stop and wait while barefoot men lead the camels onward. Closer to Delhi, pounding monsoon rains gush. The dirt road swells into a waterway. Muddy water inches its way through the Jeep floorboards, drenching my feet. The driver speeds forward, leaving a trail of waves.

By the end of the summer, I'm ready to be done with India. Dad is off on a business trip to San Francisco, and Mom drops us off at the airport. We walk into the terminal, luggage in tow, and masses of locusts fill the air. On their last gasp, locusts fly low about two feet from the ground, dive-bombing into my legs.

Swarming, squirming, dying locusts flop around on the shiny white tile floor. With each crunchy step, bug guts squish up around the edges of my new sandals and ooze between my toes. We have two hours before our plane's departure. In complete disgust, I vow never to return to India.

My sister and I joyously fly off to Bangkok and then on to Tokyo. On our last day in Tokyo, we check out of the hotel and leave our bags at the reception desk while we go shopping.

We ride the tiny elevator to the lobby of the hotel. The lower levels are offices; the hotel lobby is on the seventh floor, with the rooms on the upper stories. As the elevator door opens, I see a man's back as he faces the check-in counter; he looks familiar.

Dad turns around and sees us with a look of shock, bewilderment, and excitement; he thought we were in Europe. After Dad left India, we decided to revisit the Orient on our way home. We're at the hotel to pick up our bags, head to the airport, and fly to Hong Kong and then Hawaii.

He rides the bullet train to the airport with us, showing us photos developed in San Francisco of our summer adventure in India. I feel happy and content, surrounded by Dad's familiarity.

One split second, and we would have missed each other. Tokyo, one of the world's largest cities, an obscure hotel lobby on the 7th floor of a skyscraper; once again, I wonder about the complex web of consciousness that connects us all and the magnificent orchestration taking place. How is it that Dad and I are so intricately interwoven and connected?

LOVE, DRUGS, AND HIPPIES
1969

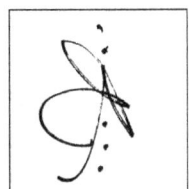

Matt and I live in a teeny cottage hidden behind a large brown shingle house. Opening the front door, a double bed, squished against two walls, consumes the room. A cramped galley kitchen separates the front room from the back room, my sewing studio—bolts of pink, blue, paisley fabric lean against the wall. Skirt, blouse, and pants patterns, drawn on heavy paper, hang on the wall—rows of colored thread line a narrow shelf. My latest creation, draped on a dress form, fills the corner.

I have never seen Dad this pissed off. Dad is so angry that he grabs Matt by the arm, shoves him outside, and slams the door. They're gone for about half an hour. I'm told Dad said, "I demand that you marry my daughter. You ruined her. Now stand up and be a man and marry her. No other man will want damaged merchandise. How the hell do you think I can marry off used goods?"

Mom sits on the one chair in the living room, looks at the bed, and cries. The bed, covered in a pure white chenille bedspread, is the site of the unmentionable. To my parents, sex is forbidden out of wedlock. I'm living an absolute scandal, what would her friends think?

My parents, firmly adhere to the prescribed rules of white male supremacy. The woman's role is to be subservient, take care of the man so that he can live his dreams. Of course, she has to be a virgin to be married off to the proper man.

Matt and I met while working at a summer camp in the mountains near Yosemite. We loved being in the woods together, hiking to remote little curves in the river where the water trickled into a perfect pool to jump in and swim. Far away from everyone, in a magical forest, the sun glistens through the trees, chirping birds. This is where we fell in love.

At the end of the summer, I decided to move to Berkeley, live with Matt, and go to fashion design school in San Francisco. I have no idea what I'm getting into when I move to Berkeley; I'm utterly oblivious to what is brewing. We've known each other for a few months, and love being around each other, but haven't discussed marriage. Our relationship isn't that far along.

We succumb to Dad's authority and decide to get married.

Years earlier, I called my parents to let them know I graduated from college. No congratulations, the only question was, did I meet a man? They had no desire to understand what I studied, my college major, or my interests. My purpose in life was to marry. On numerous occasions, my mother told me it's best to marry a rich man; that way, it's not quite so bad. She had no thought that my life could be different or better than hers. The message is clear; don't rock the boat.

My mother, held captive to tradition, believed she had no choice in life; there was no prospect of a woman living her dreams. She was educated and held a college degree in math, which is extremely rare for a woman born in 1910.

The woman's life is of little value; it is a stepping stone for the man to further himself and reach his dreams. I'm fully groomed to fulfill this role, my destiny to become a housewife and mother. The global plight of women, shockingly apparent in Iran, vividly displayed in India, magnificently curated in Switzerland, wired in my body's neural patterns.

Cosmic Inner Seeing

Neither of those roles, housewife or mother, appealed to my mother, but I'm expected to continue the tradition.

Mom's passion is a side event; being a housewife is the only path, passed down in her lineage, her DNA for millennia, and delivered to me. Her love of designing clothes was lived on the sidelines at the Country Club. Arriving a bit late, she made a grand entrance in her latest fashion. The best-dressed woman, her friends envied her creativity and style. Months or years after she strutted her outfits at the Altadena Town and Country Club, a similar design appeared on the cover of Vogue; this repeatedly happened for years. She was a maverick, a brilliant fashion designer, her finger on the pulse, ahead of the times. She never received the acclaim and money she hungered.

I started sewing when I was three; it was my only way to connect with Mom. I'm in school, attending the San Francisco School of Fashion Design, one block from Union Square. French draping, patternmaking, and sewing skills from a woman who worked in a Parisian atelier—things my mother would kill to learn. Everyone in the school is interested in haute couture and formal gowns; I'm designing Berkeley streetwear. I created two wedding dresses, one for a friend and one for myself. After a few months, I realize I'm living Mom's dream, not mine.

Where does my mother end, where do I begin?

I don't know how to find my dreams. My life was designed to serve everyone else and to put my needs and desires last. My voice is of no consequence.

Decades later, I discovered Dr. Bruce Lipton's work on how our bodies develop. As tiny children, we absorb everything in our environment. Our brains haven't developed enough to differentiate ourselves from other people. When we're six or seven, our nervous system has encoded everything from our culture to our family's fears, desires, and wants. By the time our brains can differentiate ourselves from others, everybody in our surroundings is already wired and encoded in our bodies.

My inner structure, built on everyone else's hopes and dreams, I am nowhere to be found. I'm stumbling along through life with no concept of who I am.

Trapped in circuitry passed down through the lineage, an invisible global cultural cage keeps women small, unheard, and pissed off. The internal structure, wired in everyone's body, programmed in the depths of humanity's collective unconscious, runs the show.

Out on the streets, Berkeley evolves into a riot zone, an epicenter of dissent. Chaos bubbles. Discontent with the system rises. A new vision emerges for greater equality, but it's filled with confusion and feelings of discontentment about the way things are, mixed with clashing ideologies. The pulsating frenzy of divergent cultures colliding together is strange for America.

The higher ideas of love and peace are being battled out in the streets, while even bloodier battles are happening in Vietnam. I've been against war since I was a kid, when my Dad built the first hydrogen bomb. It is a time of great internal chaos mixed with political and social unrest.

Telegraph Avenue is the hotbed of the Free Speech Movement and the best cheap Mexican restaurant in Berkeley. We go to our favorite Mexican restaurant at least once a week, stepping over spaced-out, tripping bodies to get to the front door. Nag Champa incense smoke loops and spirals, the Beatles 'All You Need Is Love' ripples out of the music store. A quivering hand reaches out, "Spare change?" The drugged-up young girl propped up against the wall asks. The smell of patchouli wafts. A wilted white daisy droops from unwashed matted hair, turning into dreadlocks. Perky breasts, feet splayed out block the sidewalk, and a hungry puppy sits in between her legs on her multi-colored long skirt.

While my inner upheaval is brewing, two realities collide in the streets. Voices bubble up from the collective, expressing the words of many. Women are speaking up, taking a stand, and demanding to be heard. I marvel at Angela Davis, Gloria Steinem, Jane Fonda, and others' ability to speak up. I don't know how they have the courage and bravery to communicate their truth. It's shocking to see women of such conviction and wisdom, conveying their thoughts openly to vast crowds of people.

Keeping quiet is so ingrained in my neural programs; I have no inner capacity to believe in myself. My childhood programming to keep quiet is still complete, intact, and running my life. There is no internal structure of my worth or my ability to trust my instincts and inner knowing. My voice bombed out of me, and it's nowhere to be found.

Along with going to school, I work at the Ski Hut on University Avenue. I spent the previous winter in Jackson Hole, Wyoming, skiing every day. I know how to talk about the camber and torque of skis, bindings, and black diamonds. The Ski Hut, headquarters for mountaineering, attracts wilderness pioneers, climbing experts, and little old ladies who live in the Berkeley Hills. The women can't drive home; police, nicknamed 'Blue Meanies,' storm the streets with their Billy clubs, bayonets, helmets with face guards, spewing mace and tear gas. In the book section of the store, we've set up a seating area, a place for people to hide during the riots. We bring tea, let them use the bathroom, and give them safety.

I sell skis, down parkas, sub-zero sleeping bags, and excellent outdoor equipment to people who love and cherish nature. On the other hand, my Dad is the chief negotiator for the Alaska pipeline, bickering about budgets for the workers' down sleeping bags and parkas. The pipeline will destroy the delicate Alaskan tundra.

Even though I'm on the outskirts of most of the chaos, my life is profoundly impacted. The Free Speech Movement, the Women's Liberation Movement, the Anti-War Movement, the Equal Rights Movement, the Black Panthers, the Gay Liberation Movement, and the Environmental Movement all confront the established patriarchal culture.

The external turmoil activates my internal angst. Pain intensifies, and music jars and clamors through my nervous system. My guts are a knotted-up mess. I feel like crap. Fire rages deep within; my head is ready to explode, and the innards of my bones scream in agony.

I know in my body, in my bones, there is nuclear radiation. The medical profession specialists tell me I am wrong; there is no way weapons-grade plutonium could be in my body. The doctors prescribe the most addictive narcotic drugs on the market. Drug me up, put me in a stupor, keep me quiet.

I'm on habit-forming narcotics with no glimmer of hope for a different reality.

I'VE GOT THE SUGAR BLUES
1971

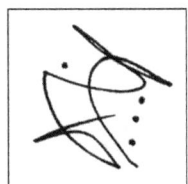

Suicidal thoughts spill out into conversations with my husband, Matt. The pain is so intense that I am ready to be done with this life. Black radioactive goo drips out my skull. A lifetime of electroshock zaps the back of my neck. My eyes burn with pressure, ready to explode. I pass out regularly. The only reality I've ever known is pain. I'm exhausted and fed up.

I've been to numerous doctors for the massive bone-eating agony I experience, but all they want to do is drug me up. Every time I mention nuclear radiation as a cause, I'm dismissed. I'm twenty-five; it's 1971.

The latest magazines have articles about hypoglycemia; I have every symptom listed. Matt contacts the endocrinologist at the hospital to set up an appointment. The doctor assures me that I cannot know what is happening in my body since I am a woman. He tells me, "I'll give you the 8-hour glucose tolerance test for your husband's peace of mind."

I passed out three times during the test. The next week, the doctor informs me that out of the thousands of cases of hypoglycemia tested at the hospital, I have the worst case he's ever seen.

My new diet consists of no sugar, no alcohol, no caffeine, and no nicotine. When I ask the doctor about what to read to educate myself, he assures me that I can't possibly understand since I'm a woman and a layperson.

I flash back to 1963, my freshman year of college biology class; I was so intrigued that I studied. Cells, neurons, dendrites, and the theory that ontogeny recapitulates phylogeny capture my interest. After the final exam, the professor called me into his office. He checked my exam three times, trying to find errors. In a class of 200 students, my test score was so high that if he graded on the curve, 199 students would've failed. In his office, he grilled me, testing to see if I had cheated. How could a girl wearing the latest fashion and a perfect hairdo understand biology? If I'd been a guy, he would've begged me to be a biology major. I assumed my place; I didn't question it. This biology exam was my first glimmer that I wasn't stupid.

Culture permeates the belief that women are foolish, inferior, and less than men. The doctor tells me to wait a few years; my hypoglycemia will become so bad that I'll turn into a diabetic and can shoot myself up with insulin.

There's no way in hell I'm going to become a diabetic; I'll do whatever it takes to heal my hypoglycemia. My inability to process sugar is inherited; my grandmother was diabetic, my mother and aunt alcoholics, and I'm hypoglycemic. All related to sugar and a lack of love, passed down in my lineage, in my DNA.

After a few days of no sugar or alcohol, sheets of grease ooze from my scalp, emitting sharp zapping razors, my hair is gooey, sickly, and smelly. I reek of nastiness, I'm a cesspool of terror, toxins, and trauma held together with fear and sugar. Putrid smells, brushing my teeth, gargling five times a day, don't touch the disgust discharging from my mouth. Black goo lines the tub after each of my four or five daily baths. I feel like crap. My exploding head is locked in the confines of my pain-wracked skull. Matt is repulsed.

After three weeks of this torture, I'm ready to give up. And then, I have a glimmer of no pain. The next day, I'm headache-free for an hour.

I can't believe I don't have a headache. Shocked to the core, after

Cosmic Inner Seeing

asking at least twenty people if they had a headache, it dawned on me that everyone doesn't always hurt. The concept of living without constant pain is so far from anything I've experienced; I don't know how to fit it into my current reality.

The headaches diminish; I have more days without pain. Being without inner torture is so foreign that it's almost scary. I have to learn how to live all over again. I know how to function with pain; a world without suffering is so unknown that, at times, I binge on sugar and retreat to the headaches because it is familiar, safe, and known. The old pattern of twenty-five years of agony runs deep; it takes a massive commitment to escape the old groove.

Why didn't anybody notice? The pattern embedded before my brain could differentiate. Passing out was a regular part of life. It never occurred to me to talk about it or to get help. It's all I knew.

I'm pissed off for weeks. How could my parents be so thoughtless and self-absorbed as not to realize that something was wrong when their daughter passed out three or four mornings a week for years? Dad was usually gone, and my mother was probably hungover. Along with rage, I feel neglected and unlovable.

At first, I wanted to be normal, like everyone else, but I decided to be the very best I could be. Since I know nothing about the world of no headaches, I realize there might be unknown realms beyond normal to explore.

I choose to live my life as fully as physically possible to make up for all the lost years of my childhood. I resolve to unleash the energy behind fear and anger and use it to propel me forward into awesome adventures, rather than drown in self-pity and pain.

Years later, I learned that sugar is four times more addictive than cocaine. Sugar is a toxin that keeps people locked in their ancient reptilian brains. Sugar perpetuates a state of fear and shuts down the higher reasoning functions. It also keeps us addicted to buying food filled with sugar.

When I was a teenager, I never understood why we were in Iran, building a sugar plantation for the Shah. Something didn't compute. You don't move from exploding bombs to growing sugar cane unless there is a hidden agenda. I finally understand the underlying motive; sugar is a cheap, highly addictive way to control the masses with fear.

Since I ceased all sugar and alcohol, the headaches and fear have diminished. Opening a space for my creativity to flow—my passion for messing around with textiles and fiber increases.

My fingers are itching to create. Weaving, spinning, dyeing, twisting fibers in new configurations, I'm in my element. Lacemaking, fingers moving quickly, fine strands of thread wrapped around bobbins, twisted over each other in a specific sequence. The intricate patterns fascinate me; somehow, lacemaking is easy, like I've done it before.

I am one of the core people of an enormous project to create multiple sprang and lace nets of sisal that encapsulate the iconic Transamerica Pyramid in San Francisco, California.

On weekends, we find a large empty parking lot and get to work. Quarter-inch rough, prickly sisal laid out, sitting on the asphalt, scooting on my butt or bending over, weaving together hundreds of pounds of rope.

Lace nets held down with 100-pound cement weights, installed with a crane, the webs soar five stories high, attached to the Transamerica Pyramid, and wrap around three expansive city blocks in the financial district of San Francisco.

The magical energy of being held envelops the sidewalks. My immense lace sculptures, some red turning into glistening gold wire, others fiber, are on display in the Transamerica Pyramid lobby and street showcases.

I participated in a fiber art sculpture installation at the de Young Museum in San Francisco's Golden Gate Park as part of the 'Rainbow Art Show' in 1974. For months, my hands stained with fabric dye helped create the primordial swamp where life emerged. Like dripping moss, fibers evoke the feeling of the beginning of life; people meander around the large, multi-colored clumps of strands, braided and carefully hung. A few years later, my unique fashions were published in a book.

Colors surge, creativity oozes, and another layer of pain surfaces.

TUNNEL OF LUMINOUS LIGHT
1973

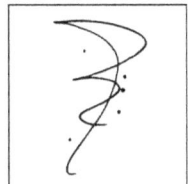

I am a walking pharmacy with all my pain pills. The pills leave a dry, sharp chemical taste in my mouth, and my head feels dull. I'm tired of these drugs that make me numb while doing nothing to heal the pain.

After radically changing my diet, the hypoglycemic headaches started to subside. Then I realized I also have migraines, sinus headaches, and pain in different parts of my head.

The migraines continue; in desperation, I go to an acupuncturist. The pungent smell of Chinese herbs mixed with incense's sweetness fills the narrow staircase leading up to Dr. Wong's office. At the top, two waiting rooms, one for men and the other for women.

Wrinkled, gray-haired women wait in straight-back wooden chairs lined against a sterile beige wall. Some knit, others read, and everyone has a sack lunch. I find an empty chair near the window overlooking Lake Merritt. Fresh from China, Dr. Wong, an expert acupuncturist and medical doctor, barely speaks English. He darts in and ducks out of the room and enters his small sanctuary. There, he meditates on whom to treat next.

Chatting with the women, I discover that even though I'm twenty-seven, I've been in pain longer than anyone in the room. We are all desperate for relief, hoping that this will work after trying countless other remedies. Dr. Wong flashes back, holding small paper packages containing fine needles. The white-haired woman with blue-gray eyes to my right is up next. His thin, delicate fingers insert needles in her face, neck, and hands; he flits out of the room. She sits calmly talking; bouncing needles distort her decades of wrinkles into astonishing patterns. Dr. Wong returns, screws the needles in deeper, and disappears.

After about three hours, it's my turn. With a wise smile, Dr. Wong holds my hand and gently places his refined fingers on my skinny wrist. His fingers, expertly checking my pulses, "Very sensitive, very sensitive," the doctor mutters with his thick Chinese accent.

He looks into my eyes and says, "Not many needles – too sensitive."

I breathe a sigh of relief; a few ultra-fine needles are screwed into my face and wrists. It feels a bit tingly, like different points connecting in my body. After a few moments, he returns to check on me. It seems like I don't have the needles in as long as the other women. The next Wednesday, the whole process is repeated.

A few weeks later, when it's my turn, I'm escorted to a small, drab room with a massage table. I change into one of those ugly pale blue gowns that open up the back. Lying on my stomach, the doctor screws a few needles in the base of my spine, back, up to my neck. Heat rises from my lower back up my spine. The warmth reaches my neck, and I feel weird, strange sensations. He quickly takes the needles out, and I go home.

Matt's so tired of my being sick; when I'm ill, he usually goes out with the guys. Tonight, he stays by my side. I've never felt like this before; over and over, I make him promise that he won't take me to the emergency room. I'm positive Western doctors will kill me. In 1973, acupuncture was almost unknown to mainstream medicine.

Cosmic Inner Seeing

In bed, the pain and heat continue to mount. No longer feeling pain, I'm gliding, soaring up a luminescent tunnel of light. The edges of the channel disperse into a vast void of darkness. I ascend further from my body, deliciously floating towards the radiance. Soothing soft rays of light welcome and caress me. I ride the shaft of light; an iridescent, opalescent archway appears before me. The light emanating from the other side of the arch is a delicious, delightful, joyful invitation.

The floor is illuminated from below; a clear line shines near my feet. An invisible barrier blocks me from stepping into another dimension. If I traverse the boundary, there is no return to my body. I long to cross over. I beg, "Can't I rest here longer with you, please?" I don't want to go back to my earthly pain-wracked body and inner horror.

No words spoken; I asked if I could please, please stay. The luminosity, joy, and celestial sounds are extraordinarily familiar and comforting. I'm told it's not my time; I can't stay. Soothing celestial music, love, and joy permeate the luminescence. I know this place; I'm HOME. Again, I plead to cross the threshold.

Asked to turn around and look back at the Earth, I see my limp, lifeless body, dissolving into the mattress, Matt sitting on the edge of the bed, holding his head in his hands.

Strings of love radiate from Matt's heart; each one has a hook, capturing a part of me, drawing and pulling me to Earth. With great hesitation and reluctance, I bid farewell and journey back to this world.

The sun streams in the window. As I awake, I hear Matt on the phone, "She's alive, she's alive, but she won't be coming to work today."

All fear of death evaporates. My demise will come at the right time. An inner knowing arises that my life is guarded and watched over. I'm unaware of the hidden agenda taking place, but I sense something profound is brewing.

BOLT OF LIGHT
1973

A few days after my near-death experience, warm sun rays fill the room on this cold, crisp fall day. The light reflects off umber walls; I'm suddenly aware of the consciousness in the cells in my left arm.

In my next breath, a luminous bolt of energy shoots up from my tailbone, electrifies my spine, and explodes out the top of my head into outer space. My consciousness catapults out beyond ordinary reality. Incandescent air; colors appear brighter, fuller, and have more depth and substance. Each cell is alive; each one is conscious.

I look up, and I see inside my husband's body. Out the window, the trees display magnificent shimmering auras.

On the street, a woman walking towards me looks like a skeleton, similar to the bones painted on costumes during the Day of the Dead in Mexico. I wonder if she's going to die soon. It's unnerving to see neural circuitry inside strangers' bodies. It's 1973; I'm twenty-seven.

Back home, I feel nothing, no connection, no attachment; no I own this sensation - everything is foreign as if I've never seen it before. On my loom is a partially woven blue and purple shawl I am making for my mother for Christmas. My large lace sculpture hangs near the balcony door, once hung in the lobby of the Transamerica

Pyramid in San Francisco. I recognize everything, yet there is no link, no ownership.

Matt's favorite song, *Angie*, by The Rolling Stones, blasts. He walks in from the sunroom; usually, my heart opens when I see Matt; today, I wonder who he is. Energetically, he has a sign on his forehead that says 'husband.' I have no emotional connection with him. A stranger in my body and a foreigner in my world, nothing is the same as it was before. I'm a witness, a bystander observing my home and life.

Two days ago, I returned from being denied access to the pearly gates, and now, I'm transported into a radically different reality. Lights stream, and I'm carried into multiple unknown dimensions. Not drug-induced; it was not like getting stoned or drunk and then feeling better in a day or two, I want to revert to normal. Matt wonders when his wife will return.

BOOK 2

EXPLORING THE UNKNOWN

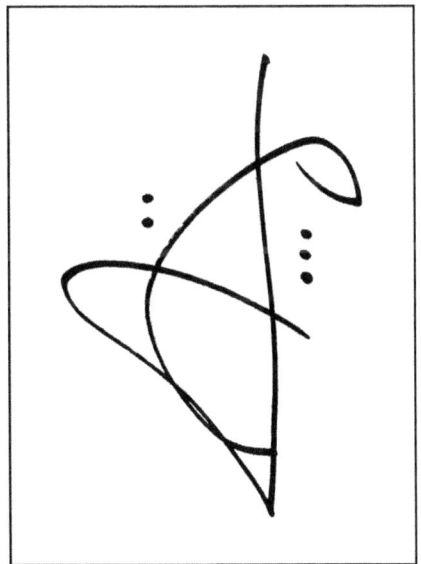

SPONTANEOUS AWAKENING
1973

The utter shock of seeing, knowing, feeling, and hearing multiple states of consciousness all at the same time, some filled with love, others oozing terror, is unnerving, overwhelming, and at times frightening. I feel so alone. I have no one to talk to, nowhere to turn. It is too scary to speak of; my actions and the tiny bits I talk about are daunting to those around me.

Deep in my bones, I know what I'm experiencing is accepted in other cultures. I remember the temples in India, and they bring me peace. Whether my certainty emanates from ancient temple carvings or some remote memories, I know I am not crazy.

The one thing I know for sure is to keep quiet.

Every day life is a mess. The simple task of trying to function in the world – go to work, walk down the street, buy food – is arduous. The changes in my nervous system are readily apparent everywhere.

Fluorescent lights in the grocery store flicker, triggering my nervous system. Can I survive in the store long enough to buy food? I'm starving; I have to eat. Tightly gripping the shopping cart, moving as fast as possible, I grab a few essentials. By the time I hit the checkout stand, I'm reeling. If there's no line, I usually make it out of the store with a few essential items.

On one visit, I blacked out at the cheese counter. When I slowly open my eyes, I am in a cold room propped against a blue plastic crate. I look up and hanging from metal beams lining the ceiling are sharp, stainless steel hooks holding large, blood-red carcasses. While unconscious, I was moved to the cold storage of the meat department. The last thing I remember, I was at the cheese counter, and my body slid down the glass onto the floor like a clump of whipped butter swirling off a stack of hotcakes.

On other days, I'm slumped on the floor like a limp bag of beans. The breakfast aisle is the worst. Have you ever seen kids acting up in the cereal aisle? They are responding to the subliminal messages, screaming, "Buy me." Advertising agencies, paid vast fortunes, use color and graphics to stimulate specific parts of the brain and nervous system. Man-made manipulation overwhelms my nervous system, and I collapse. Back home, I'm disoriented putting the groceries away. That night, Matt found ice cream dripping between the plates in the cupboard and peanut butter in the freezer.

Huge doors open to the expansive library at UC Berkeley, tall windows line the walls, and high ceilings soar. Beliefs, theories, and ideologies ooze out of books, slide down the stacks, gather momentum, cascade through the library, and engulf the glistening floor. It's like all the characters in the books jump off the pages and rush to greet me. A tidal wave, drowning in a sea of vivid personalities and conflicting thoughts, I faint.

When I walk into a record store, musical notes cascade in waves and swirl around my body. Never cleared, a cloud of previously played music hangs in the air; rock, classical, country, pop, and jazz all clang together in the most horrific jangle of vibrations assaulting my body. The cacophony of sounds creates chaos, my bombarded nervous system goes into shock, and I crumple up on the floor.

I finally realized there is no turning back. During the explosion out of the top of my head, a rearrangement took place. I can't return to the state I was in previously. Radical, permanent change, I'm catapulted into other realms, with one foot still in 3-D reality. Numerous layers of stratum are all jumbled together in one big, unknown mess.

Cosmic Inner Seeing

Each dimension has particular ways of perceiving reality, unique frequencies, and a distinct twist on how things work. On other dimensions, space and time aren't linear like in 3-D; everything happens in the now. Linear time is a third-dimensional construct used to order our reality.

Beyond limited 3-D perception, my seeing is fluid, shifting between axons and dendrites, neurons bound together in patterns formed in early childhood trauma, floating into subatomic particles, and then flowing on to the angelic realms. Imagine an anatomy book, with multiple pages of transparent paper, each one showing a different layer of your body - your nervous system, skeletal system, organs and veins, and arteries.

My senses are rarified and intensified—a conglomeration of sensual input shifts throughout the day. At one moment, my vision changes, and the trees shimmer in iridescent colors, surrounded by golden halos; the colors of the grass intensify like the psychedelic paintings strewn around town.

It takes me decades to sort through and unravel the dimensions and figure out what is what, like fitting together a cosmic multidimensional jigsaw puzzle.

A neurological shift in consciousness occurred that was not recognized in American culture in 1973. I'm living in Berkeley, the most far-out city in the country, the hotbed of the flower child, the Free Speech Movement, and anti-war protests; what I'm experiencing is beyond the most radical consciousness.

Not only can I sense and feel my immediate surroundings, but my awareness of all humanity and world events intensifies. I'm continuously bombarded on all sides about the global crisis.

In the '70s, there was no Google to search for answers. Yoga is virtually unknown in the USA; quantum physics is relegated to a few, and spiritual awakenings are not a part of everyday culture.

Luckily, I've lived in Iran, Switzerland, and India and know that various cultures view reality in divergent ways. Memories from India waft through my consciousness, leaving a small trail of sanity.

About four years after this experience, a friend told me she thought of me whenever she read the book *Kundalini* by Gopi Krishna. Laid out in print, I read about everything I'm experiencing right before my eyes—wave upon wave of relief echoes through my body. I'm not crazy; I experienced a spontaneous kundalini awakening. Awakenings of this magnitude are extremely rare. In the East, these states of consciousness are sought after; people spend years, sometimes lifetimes, of austere practice, preparing to awaken their kundalini.

Kundalini, in Hindu and Tantric traditions, is a form of divine feminine energy located at the base of the spine, the power of awakening, and evolutionary transformation. This is the energy propelling self-awareness and spiritual development.

I'm very thankful for Krishna's book, yet I'm not a man living in India. He talks about how his wife takes care of him when he is in an altered state. The American culture is not set up for spiritual awakenings, especially for women. Men are granted the luxury of being mystical or geniuses, but women are labeled crazy.

A few years later, I met a woman who also had a spontaneous Kundalini awakening; however, she told her kids about her experiences. They got scared and had her locked up in a mental institution. She was tied up in a straitjacket, given electroshock treatments, and drugged. When I met the dear woman, she was barely functioning. My heart went out to her. Her children were making sure they kept her brain under control. She didn't have the support she needed or the inner knowing to stay quiet, so her life became a living hell.

My rigorous childhood top-secret training served me well. Keeping quiet saved me from being doped up, tortured, and imprisoned in a mental institution.

Nowhere to turn, I'm without a rudder, a guide, or a map. I have to figure this out on my own. Kundalini continues to surge through my body, reconstructing my life. My cosmic inner seeing leads the path into the unknown.

ENDINGS
1974

Matt wants to be with the woman he married; she doesn't exist. My radical neurological shift in consciousness created a new person. Over time, differences magnify, and nine months after my awakening, we divorce.

Seven years later, Matt and I are still energetically connected. Walking down the street in Berkeley, something will trigger Matt's memory of me, a building, one of our favorite places, a particular color, and I will call him. Sometimes I think of him, and he calls me. We agreed to meet in person to understand what's happening. Are we to be together? I fly from Aspen, Colorado, to Berkeley, California.

As we talk, a vast pillar of light descends around us—a force field, like when Captain Kirk says, 'Beam me up, Scottie' in Star Trek. Surrounded by shimmering frequencies, a laser of light dissolves the cords and connections between us; at that moment, we are separate and complete.

That night we celebrated our ending at our favorite restaurant—a small place on Ashby Avenue, with only six tables, curried chicken the specialty. Synchronicity at play, sitting at the table next to us, are two friends who were with us when we met, were at our engagement party, attended our wedding, and are now present to witness our completion. That was the last time I saw Matt.

Newly alone, I moved and quit my job at the Ski Hut. The guy who replaced me was paid more on his first day of work than I received after five long years. I ask my boss why, and he very clearly states that men are worth more; they get paid higher wages.

It's difficult to function in 3-D reality when I'm connected to so many unknown, mysterious dimensions. Bit by bit, I slowly and systematically shut down my inner seeing; I create blinders to eradicate the light. Inside my body, it looks like pulling down a shade to block out the sun. I no longer see inside strangers' bodies or pass out in the grocery store or libraries. My sensitivity and seeing are greatly diminished. At times, I am sad that I shut down, but I need to operate in the world and earn a living.

I still hear the type of physical abuse people have suffered. Unhealed sexually abused women have an undercurrent of terror, a high-pitched scream in their voices. Every word is an outcry of bone-chilling horror, like claws scraping rusted metal. It's shocking to me that other people can't hear their shrieking cries for help. Globally, one in two women will be sexually assaulted in her lifetime. Social events are excruciating; there are usually a few unhealed sexually abused women present. Being in a group of yapping women is torture; my solution is to become a recluse.

Ever since that day in Berkeley, when the energy shot up my spine, there have been times when Shakti pounds her way through my body. Shakti is the primordial cosmic energy, divine female energy responsible for creation, an agent of change, and the source of both matter and physical energy. The pulsating energy pushes up, crisscrossing back and forth around my spine, reaching for my head, and it is excruciating. Headaches usually accompany the throbbing pain. The energy surging through my body is so much higher and more powerful than I am; my only path is total surrender.

At this time, yoga is almost unknown in the States; I certainly know nothing about yoga, Shakti, or Kundalini. Similar to Kundalini yoga, but spontaneously erupting, Shakti thunders her way through my body. My body moves in strange contortions, known as kriyas; my hands impulsively create sacred mudras or hand gestures. Short, rapid breaths take over as my body undulates on the floor, dislodging ancient blocks and debris—my breathing shifts. Short bursts in and out of my nose, long, slow belly breaths, arms flying, fingers moving in sacred patterns, my body uncoils. I hide, not wanting anyone to see what is happening. I don't want to be locked up.

Defying patriarchal views that Shakti needs to be induced up the spine, my Shakti deliciously seeps and storms down my legs. She lusciously saturates my body with her tingling force of evolution.

An emerging realization starts to dawn on me of the two main forces playing out in my body: weapons-grade plutonium and Kundalini. Man-made plutonium-239, the active ingredient in nuclear warfare, designed at its core to annihilate, kill, and destroy, wired in my nervous system, hides in my bones and resides in every cell.

Each is different from the other, yet they synthesize to create a sensitive, unique combination of experiences in my body. The spiritual insights brought on by the Kundalini awakening have had a tremendous impact on my coming to terms with bombs, radiation, and war. All the dimensions of reality open to bring me tremendous insights about life, death, and seeing who we are.

The craziness associated with plutonium is different from the madness of Kundalini. The first lunacy is brought on by toxicity, fear, and domination; the second is the derangement brought on by divine rapture, joy, and being drunk with the beloved; such a weird tapestry, woven together to create this life.

Dodging the lunatic frequencies of modern-day life, I escape into the remote regions of the world.

MT. EVEREST CLEAN-UP TREK
1976

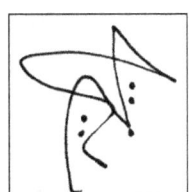

Teetering on my rented bicycle, I'm following Stan as he darts through a narrow, winding marketplace in Kathmandu. Prayer flags wave in the breeze, Nepalese rope incense fills the air, both sides of the lane have small shops with used camping equipment for sale, and small stalls sell strange assortments of things.

My bike is wobbly; I'm trying to keep up with Stan, but he's way ahead of me. We're searching for twenty-two large cloth bags with over-the-shoulder straps. Bags to use for picking up trash. He is the leader, and I'm the assistant leader on the world's first Mt. Everest clean-up expedition.

I met Stan on my first day working at an international travel agency specializing in trips to remote places. Walking down steep stairs to the basement offices, Stan and I say, Hi, in the narrow staircase. A flash of lightning sparked between us, and an instant connection occurred. The next day, he left on his first trip to Nepal to lead a trek to Mt. Everest.

One and a half years later, we're riding rickety bicycles in Kathmandu. To celebrate my thirtieth birthday, I'm here for a fabulous adventure. This clean-up trek is a chance to clean up the environment, a passion of mine since childhood. To clear mankind's toxic debris covering the beauty and awe of pristine nature. It's also a time for inner reflection on what's next in my life.

Everywhere we go, people say, Namaste. Clasped hands at the heart, a slight bow, the Sanskrit word Namaste, means 'I bow to the Lotus within.'

Sherpas carry large hand-woven baskets filled above the brim with food, tents, sleeping bags, and everything needed for twenty-eight days for this group of twenty-two trekkers. A strap on their forehead, a basket perched on curved backs. Chickens in handmade cages cackle, resting on top of the enormous load. Yaks follow along, loaded with supplies; everything we need comes from Kathmandu.

Every day, gaining altitude, at night, we sleep at lower elevations to acclimatize while ascending the valley and mountains. At 10,000', we walk through a rhododendron forest filled with white blossoms; soft, silky petals flicker in the breeze. A luscious, sublime scent fills the air. I dream of rowing a boat down the Grand Canyon, as I step through this magical wonderland of beauty.

A few days later, we're crossing the Dudh Kosi River on a rope bridge. The rumbling white water, strewn with massive boulders, looks like it's a gazillion feet below these skinny wooden slats. The bridge swings in the wind, and little planks of wood, some missing, are held together with thin rope. In absolute panic, I'm holding on for dear life, using every inch of courage to get to the other side.

I flash back to five years ago, on a cold winter's day, when I broke my leg skiing in Jackson Hole, Wyoming. Bandanna over my mouth, the wind chill was 30 below. My ski caught an edge; the frozen binding didn't release. Boot top fracture, my right foot, and ski faced backward.

The doctor said my leg looked like a saltine cracker in a plastic wrapper, the cracker pounded into tiny bits. My bones shattered, and he said I probably would never walk again. I did everything in my power to heal my broken leg. Now, I'm here trekking in Nepal. Yes, I tell myself, I have the strength and stamina to make it across this terrifying rope bridge.

My fanny pack is filled with prescription drugs; I don't dare take a step without them. Massive pain, still undiagnosed. My narcotics keep me going past the pain. Even though it's dangerous at high altitudes, it's the only way I can manage.

The majesty of the land brings peace to my pain-wracked body. Waves of dignity and compassion flow through the country, envelope the trees, and permeate the air—such a stark contrast to my bombs and nuclear warfare upbringing. For decades, the winds have carried prayers, Om Mani Padme Hum, the Sanskrit, "Praise to the Jewel in the Lotus." Mani walls of carved rock guide the path, filled with messages of love and respect for each other and all of humanity. The land exudes tranquility and peace I've never experienced before.

Smiling women, Sherpanis, carry enormous heavy baskets, trek by laughing and giggling, enjoying every moment, as we Westerners gasp for every breath. Deep belly breaths, slow, steady pace, trekking further into the glorious mountains. Jaw-dropping vistas, mountain peaks inching their way to the heavens, and prayer flags send blessings throughout the land. My dreams of being on the river sparkle through the valleys like prayer flags billowing in the wind.

We arrived at Tengboche Monastery at 12,687 feet (3,867 meters) after trekking up and down for hours. Everything is so known; it feels like I have been here before. I've been stepping on unstable ground for days and sprained my ankle on a flat campsite. I wonder if the familiarity of the place invites me to want to stay. The humongous, luminous snow-capped mountains create a majestic refuge.

My foot is too swollen in the morning to squeeze into my boot; I'm left behind. My tent, pitched next to the Tengboche Monastery walls, has sweeping views of the spectacular range of mountains before me. From dawn to dusk, monks sit a few feet away, spinning prayer wheels, deep chanting swirls, enveloping my tent. Tall brass Tibetan horns emit resounding tones played by monks in long saffron robes; clanging metal, drum beats, and chanting exude from the monastery. I'm at home, safely protected, and looked after. I wonder how many lifetimes I've been a monk, how many eons I've spent in meditation.

An inner call beckons; beyond what I know, a repeating vision of me rowing a boat down the Grand Canyon appears. A far-out fantasy, I'm a skinny chick who knows nothing about rowing a boat or rivers. Back in school, I wasn't allowed to play sports; I was too frail. If I told anyone my dreams, they would laugh, saying it's impossible.

On the second day, a runner arrives with a sweet note from Stan and a small tin of peanut butter. The stunning beauty, force, and energy of the mountains nurture my body. Away from Western consumerism, advertising, and man-made reality, nature infuses my life. The mountains exude mystery, magic, and ancient wisdom. There's magnetism, a pull to embrace and become one with nature.

After a few days, the swelling has gone down enough to jam my foot into my hiking boot, so Tensing, my excellent Sherpa guide, and I head off. The first night we came to his village, Pangboche at 13,074 feet (3,985 m), so I stayed with Tensing's family in their home.

Yaks, chickens, goats, and sheep live on the first floor. Upstairs is one sizable smoky room with a blackened ceiling. A fire in the center of the room is used for cooking and to keep the family warm. Tiny windows allow in some light while thick walls keep out the bitter cold. There is no running water. White thumbprints on dark wooden shelves decorate the kitchen area. Shiny copper pots, in a row, long-handled, large metal ladles hang on a nail. An old wooden churn rests in the corner, ready to make the next batch of yak butter—a picture of pure, simple beauty.

I feel honored to stay in Tensing's home and to meet his family. We eat dal, or lentils, and the most delicious potatoes I've ever tasted. I sleep on the floor with three generations of family. In the morning, we head off to catch up with the others.

Reunited with the group in Lobuche, celebrating at the teahouse, *chang*, a type of beer or tea with salty, rancid yak butter, is served. That night, *chang* in our bellies, the Sherpas and Sherpanis sing and dance around the glowing embers of the campfire, inviting us to join in. I can't keep up, gasping for air, my feet slowly move to the rhythm. Looking up, it feels like I can touch the stars.

In Lobuche at 16,200 feet, I am cleaning up a small compound. An older Nepalese woman stops and watches me, then looks at the area around her home. I observe her brain making new connections. She looks at the space I have cleaned, then at the trash around her house. For eons, until foreigners came to scale Mt. Everest, everything in the Nepalese culture at this elevation was either biodegradable or something precious like jewelry. Insensitive foreigners bring in trash and litter the countryside with stupidity, disrespect, and toxic Western ways.

When she was a small girl, there was no trash, and now the place is strewn with silver chewing gum wrappers, small plastic film canisters, the thick plastic metallic packages film comes in, and used toilet paper—in 1976, digital cameras didn't exist. After she watches me for a while, she bends over and picks up the garbage around her house. The context of the woman's life did not include the concept of waste. It did not occur to her to pick up the garbage. The people on the clean-up trek collected trash from forty-three different countries.

On some level, I've always felt like trash, that I'm not worthy, and I need to hide to be accepted. Like the Nepalese lady with no concept of trash, I had no knowledge that I could clear up the toxic thought structures and unconscious layers that ran my life.

I'm astonished when we reach Gorak Shep, at 17,083 feet (5,207 m); the ground is mauve, light lavender, pink glistening sand. My head spins, calculating the movement of the earth's tectonic plates to create the upward thrust of Mount Everest, Lhotse, and Nuptse towering above fine, delicate, shimmering sand. The minuscule importance of man during the lifetime of the Earth is humbling.

At the Kala Patthar summit, 18,513 feet (5643M), the views of Everest are spectacular. The white rolling plume on the summit shifts, revealing the peak. Chills run up my spine, viewing the tallest point on Earth, I feel so blessed and alive. And yet, my body is aching to stand on tiptoe and peer over the Himalayas into Tibet. I long to walk the high Tibetan plains.

Two days later, a loud crack whips, ricocheting through the Himalayas. The Earth rumbles; sitting in my tent in the afternoon sun, I watch four avalanches slide off the face of Mt. Everest. With a deep roar, vast slabs of snow crack loose, and massive torrents of frozen snow boulders tumble, gaining momentum, thundering down Everest. Billows of snow clouds envelop huge areas of the mountain. Even though our tents are a safe distance away, it feels like the avalanches will engulf me in a second. The peaks turn golden, then pink as the sun sets, and a cold wind blows through camp.

It's too hard to stand up, bend over, and pick up trash. I'm creeping on my belly, gasping for breath, picking up other people's garbage. I was thrilled at the opportunity to be the assistant leader on the 1st Mt. Everest Clean-up Trek. Now I wonder, what in me feels compelled to clean up other people's rubbish?

When I was five, and Dad came home from building the first hydrogen bomb, my question was, "Who will clean up the mess?" Now, Dad is in Saudi Arabia, in charge of the world's largest construction project, building pipelines and oil refineries. Between toxic nuclear radiation and gasoline, my father's handiwork impacts life on a global scale.

Does my unworthiness stem from feeling responsible for the mess my Dad is creating? Maybe if I clean up enough of other people's crap, then I'll feel worthy.

AFRICAN ELEPHANTS IN KATHMANDU
1976

Skin-on-skin body heat is the best way to keep warm in freezing weather at high elevations. For twenty-eight days, two sleeping bags zipped together, our two naked bodies cuddled. We reek. The tiny plates of tepid washing water, delivered to our tent every morning, are an inferior substitute for a luxurious, long, hot shower.

Back in Kathmandu, after twenty-eight days of trekking, Stan and I couldn't agree on who would get the first shower. We jump in the shower together. I marvel at the rivulets of dirt flowing down his hairy legs, creating puddles of mud around his feet. We scrub each other's backs; hot running water never felt so luscious. We clean up and meet some friends for dinner.

Meandering down Kathmandu's dirt lanes, winding between stone houses, we come to The Chimney, the renowned Russian restaurant. The open, copper-shafted fireplace blazes, filling the room with a warm glow and a cozy, enchanted feeling. We meet up with our friends, Gina and Ted, over hot steaming bowls of delicious Russian borscht or beet soup.

A German man walks up to the table and says, "Namaste" to Ted. Peter has just arrived from South Africa, where he has been living and filming for the past few years.

I flashback; everything tumbles into place. I know of this man, Peter. Two years before, in Berkeley, California, Lee came for a visit. Even though we lived halfway around the world from each other, Lee is one of my best friends. Lee's next stop is London, to present her latest film to the Queen of England. We did some serious shopping. We wanted to capture the perfect look of an American filmmaker showing her African footage to the Queen.

I hear of her dream to travel to Nepal and the exquisite details of her relationship with her lover, Peter. Lee moved to Africa to film wildlife, met Peter, and they fell in love.

Back in Africa, one day in 1975, Lee was in Rwanda, out in the savanna filming a herd of elephants. These elephants are usually very docile and safe. This day, something out of the ordinary occurs; they stampede. Lee is connected to the camera's large, heavy battery pack and cannot escape. She spent the last moments of her life filming elephants charging straight towards her. Learning of her death, I had a deep desire to see Lee's movie, to form closure, and to get a taste of what she experienced. The thought dissolved and never arose again. At the time, I was living in Berkeley, happily married, weaving, creating art and lace, with no desire to visit Nepal.

Lee's dream was to travel to Nepal. Here I am in Kathmandu, and Lee's lover walks up to our table. Peter smiles, we exchange a few words, and I watch his brain compute. He realizes I'm Lee's friend. Peter invites us to see Lee's movie, showing the next night at the British Embassy.

In a dimly lit room of the British Embassy in Kathmandu, I gasp as the dust flies; the ground shakes, trunks swaying side-to-side, trumpeting sounds echo, the elephant's charge. Huge ears flap in the wind, snorts, roars, rumbles, and giant elephants lumber closer. I imagine the baby elephant's knee in her chest, crushing the last breath out of my dear friend Lee's life. I feel moved, a completion occurred.

The human fragility and the intricate workings of the cosmic play of this life are humbling. A German man arrives at a Russian restaurant in Nepal, and he invites Americans to the British Embassy to see a movie filmed in Africa. What a plethora of people and countries are involved in this marvelous synchronistic completion. What is happening behind the scenes in this human drama?

What are the complex components of the universe necessary to line up a group of people, seven countries, and this magic moment to come together? What are the cosmic forces at play? I put out the intention of the desire to see this movie two years prior. At the time, I had no inclination to go to Nepal. Here I am in Nepal, a place that Lee wanted to visit. Did her desire help to pull me to Kathmandu? Am I living out some of her wishes? At times, I wonder where I end and others begin. I think we're living in one big interconnected cosmic soup—quantum entanglement manifesting on Earth.

We're all connected.

While in Nepal, I keep sensing a connection like a web. Is it Indra's web, the Buddhist and Hindu philosophy to describe interconnectedness, a net with jewels or pearls at each point of contact? The quantum physics theory of nonlocality? Synchronicity? Or some other phenomenon? Whatever the explanation, I'm in awe of this magical world.

THE RIVER
1976

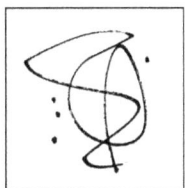

I pull up to an old farmhouse on a large, scruffy patch of dry land. Tents and tarps cover the dirt. Wooden oars, rubber rafts, ammo cans, black rubber bags, and life vests cascade from the barn. The outhouse is hidden behind the barn, and an outdoor shower is hooked up to a bulky wooden water tower. The water heats in the sun and provides enough liquid to hose down a bushel of boatmen. I am in Angels Camp, California, learning how to be a white-water river guide.

Stunned, not knowing what to expect, I walked inside. Dishes covered with caked-on scraps of food overflow the sink. Inside the toilet is a thick black rim, pee runs down the outside—a saggy living room couch, covered with food stains and cigarette holes. Sweaty T-shirts mingle with the scent of moldy food and musty, damp towels. A few bare mattresses, with sleeping bags thrown on top, line the floor in each of the two bedrooms. Sleeping bags spread throughout the house and spilled out to the porch.

River talk, expressions I've never heard, places I can't fathom, fill the air. An unfamiliar language describes the hydraulics of the ebb and flow of the river. Every rapid and sandy beach has a name; every boulder is etched into memory. Words swirl around me, fueling flames of anticipation and fascination.

About forty yummy, tan, hard-body guys, all camped out in this house and grounds. The boatmen are standoffish, eyeing me with suspicion. I'm the only female. Who is this thirty-year-old divorced woman, ponders the twenty-year-old boatmen? Hearing I've spent the last three months in Nepal trekking with one of their most revered head boatmen, Stan, an opening occurs.

This house isn't filled with a bunch of crass-talking dudes getting drunk. What started as a Boy Scout leader taking his scouts on river trips grew into a world-class boating company. Several boatmen have known each other since childhood, almost like a family, more like a tribe. A distinct breed, who has a passion for water, faces fear and encounters personal river initiations. Every night, stories flow about the perils and excitement of distant rivers. I want to row all of these exotic, treacherous water passages, and eventually, I do.

It's hot; I'm in my cut-offs, flip-flops, and a tank top. The odor of oil-based paint intensifies in the heat as I paint and shellac oars and stack them upright against the barn to dry in the baking sunlight. I need both hands to pick up and move around a 30-pound oar; I've got no arm muscles.

The boathouse smells like used tires. Each boat was pumped up and examined to make sure it would hold air. Patching minor rips or leaks, making sure they stick. Rows of camp stoves were cleaned, checked for missing parts, fueled up, primed, and tested. Faulty equipment, out in the wilderness, can be dangerous. Every precaution is needed to ensure the safety of the passengers.

My boss George, wants me to pack food, do bookkeeping, answer phones, and do jobs he will pay me to do. I refuse. I'm here to learn to row, not stuck inside doing women's work. I work for free for weeks, eat as cheaply as possible, scrape by, and somehow survive.

I'm an outsider trying to burst down the door into a man's world. Until I become licensed, I have no way to earn money. I have no safety net, yet, I'm determined to be a boatman.

My every move was judged and scrutinized. One by one, the

boatmen warm up to me. I learn how to haul a trailer behind a large truck. Half hitches, a boating knot, become my friends. I'm not making lace; I am tying down gear, pulling my full weight on the rope. I started to master how to rig a boat. Everything needs to be secure if the boat flips; I don't want lunch to float downriver.

Most of the one-day trips on the Stanislaus River have four or five boats, each with about four passengers and one boatman. On some trips, there's extra space in one of the rafts, so I come along and practice.

Every day is humbling. The sun beats down; the cold river splashes relief on my skinny, spindly, aching wrists and arms. My fingers, skilled at making lace, sewing, and weaving, burn from clenching down on oars, and calluses build. Arm muscles develop. It takes a lot of practice to build up the strength and skill to move the raft through moving water. The boat probably weighs a couple of thousand pounds; by the time you add in the passenger's weight, the water jumping in from the river, the boat gets heavy.

One day, Amy arrives. At last, I'm not the only female learning the ways of the river. In my five years on the river, Amy and I have been on two trips together; other than that, I'm always the only female boatman.

The guys muscle their way through the rapids and down the river. The only way for me to be a boatman is to learn to read the water and surrender to the river. To be considered an equal, I have to excel; otherwise, I'm just a chick, not taken seriously. Like rowing a boat upstream, against the current, it's not easy. On my second try, I passed the rowing exam on the Stanislaus River.

River stories of the Rogue, in Grants Pass, Oregon, tickle my mind, and boating season on the Rogue is just beginning. I jump in my car and head for Oregon.

Every river has a different system of licensing boatmen. To become certified on the Rogue, I need to pass two exams. A written test administered by the State of Oregon, including flora and fauna, history, river etiquette and safety, and the rowing exam is judged and graded by a certified examiner.

I'm short on cash to pay the fee for the rowing exam. In exchange for rowing the supply boat for a five-day kayak school trip, the kayak school director will grade me on every rapid. The head of the kayak school is a licensed, certified rowing examiner.

The kayaking school staff keenly eye me; it's obvious some of them want nothing to do with a woman rowing a boat on 'their' river. The dude who outfits the boat for me to row doesn't want a woman to pass. The sabotaged, crappy, old, patched-up boat is soggy, doesn't hold air, and is almost impossible to maneuver. The bent, twisted, off-center frame has oarlocks; I trained on oars with pins where I can lean my full body weight into the oar to maneuver through the rapids. With oarlocks, the action and strength take place in the wrists. I was given thick, heavy, bulky oars, used on high-volume rivers like the Grand Canyon. Thinner, lightweight oars are typically utilized on technical rivers like the Rogue.

The dude has done everything in his power to ensure my failure. If I speak up, I'll be labeled weak, a woman, not capable. Panic surges through my body; I have to pass this exam. Every morning, I pump up my boat and double-check every rope, every knot.

Delicate fingers clutch thick, round wooden oar handles, and my wrists scream, keeping the oars at the right angle to maneuver my boat. If the oar slips, it slices through the water like a knife rather than a paddle. On every significant rapid, tears stream down my face, muscles roar, and my slender arms and wrists finesse the massive barge through the turbulent water. Each morning, my fingers are cramped in a circle; someone has to massage my fingers so they can move.

At a slow part of the river, the kayakers practice their rolls. One kayaker completes a masterful roll; his ego puffs up in enormous proportions as he paddles downriver. A few moments later, a gnarly hand rises out of the river, scoops up the kayaker, flips him over, and retreats into the gently flowing river. Sputtering water, scrambling for air, the kayaker squirms out of his kayak and limps to shore. The river, in her wisdom, brought his ego down a notch, castrating his arrogance, so he'd have the humility to learn her magic. On the bank, the kayaking instructor and I look at each other and smile; the twinkle in his eye says it all.

I passed both tests, license in hand, I'm an official boatman on the Rogue.

Early morning mist starts to burn off; the sun rises over the ridge, and the calm river sparkles. At the river's edge, five boats and five boatmen line up, ready for passengers. Six days of food for twenty passengers and gear packed in waterproof ammo cans fill the back of the boats. My boat is the last one the hesitant passengers choose; only guys are fit to row a boat. One family almost forfeited their vacation; they didn't want a female guide.

It's 1976 before it is 'in' to be in shape. Nike hasn't sold women on having muscles yet, so we are expected to be rather helpless, weak, and dependent. Who on earth would want to get into a skinny chick's boat? Here I am, sun-bleached hair, tanned, muscular body, turquoise bikini, knife strapped around my waist, knife tip tied to my leg, and sunglasses.

Like event planning, we discover who our passengers are and map out the entire event, from food, lunch stops, and camping places, to give everyone the most magical, fun trip imaginable. Many campsite choices include a natural, carved-out rock water slide ending in a waterfall and a hike up a lush canyon. Or the spot where people can swim through the rapids, then walk upstream and do it again, or high cliffs to dive into the river. We have an abundant food budget and a layover day for this trip.

Today's passengers are from Hollywood, well-known actors, a director, and a therapist. Leaving behind their everyday lives, schedules, and watches, stripped of the known, familiar clothes are exchanged for the vulnerability of a bathing suit. We are in charge of the passengers' lives for the next six days, their food, safety, where to camp, and their emotional well-being.

On the first night, fine wine accompanies grilled fresh salmon. The river displays her magic. Osprey pluck salmon out of the river, great blue herons glide to their nests high in the trees, deer come to the river at sunset to drink, and brown bears play at the water's edge.

By the third day, the city's frantic energies start to dissolve, and the passengers relax into the beauty of nature. An opening occurs, safe in the competent hands of experienced guides, and passengers rekindle their love of life. At the river's edge, baby mergansers, fluffy reddish-brown with white patches, trail their mothers. By the end of boating season, fuzzy down transforms into feathers, necks elongate, and the ducks take flight.

While the passengers set up their tents, I sneak out to pick blackberries and make a delicious berry cobbler in the Dutch oven over the hot campfire coals. My full-length dress flutters in the breeze, and a wildflower bouquet graces the plastic folding table. We surprise the passengers with hand-cranked homemade ice cream.

A canyon wren chirps while an osprey flies overhead, caught in the orange disk of the setting sun. At dusk, the smell of the canyon walls shifts as the air currents move upstream. The warm musky fragrance of the earth exudes as the soil's heat moves up the ravine's surface, and the ground cools down for the night. The aroma and the song of the canyon wren enhance the closing of daylight—the long silver, gold, and taupe rays of sunlight glide across the silky smooth midnight blue river.

Mid-trip, we stay at the same campsite for two nights. The passengers explore and relax. Dinner is a rack of lamb, roasted over an open fire. We tie our oars together to create a sweat lodge, covered in tarps, next to a dipping pool in the river.

I always sleep away from the passengers, out in the open, embraced by the moon and stars. One morning, I opened my eyes and there, standing above me, one front leg on each side of my shoulders, his nose a few inches from my face. Looking me straight in the eyes is an alpha male deer, a ten-point buck. Waves of joy and delight fill my body. We look in each other's eyes for who knows how long, and he slowly backs up and disappears into the wilderness. I am so happy. I love deer, always have. When I was a kid, and we went camping, I used to collect lichen and feed the deer out of the palm of my hand. I feel so blessed to have this massive animal connect with me in such a profound way.

The river teaches me her mysteries, and I learn physics, the laws of nature and the universe, along with surrender, humility, fear, courage, strength, and perhaps most important of all, the secrets of wave and flow. The wave smoothly slides and ripples through my body, caressing every cell as its undulating flow electrifies and enlivens. The Shakti flowing through my body finally meets her match in the intensity of the massive rapids on the river.

We guide passengers not only into the unknown wilds but also into uncharted internal territory. Riding life-threatening rapids is scary; it brings up all kinds of repressed, hidden fears. I'm the one the passengers turn to when terror arises. I learn group dynamics, how to ease tense situations.

As I approach enormous rapids, a wall of fear arises that almost leaves me paralyzed. Every day on the river, every rapid, I face fear, building up my inner courage. Over time, I discovered how to transform the fear and place it behind me, giving me the power to guide my boat through the thundering, gigantic rapids with finesse. On the days of the biggest rapids, on top of my turquoise bikini, I wear a mid-thigh length kimono, covered with blue and white waves, cinched down with my orange Mae West life jacket.

The water becomes silky smooth at the top of a rapid, right before it cascades down a narrow path. The bigger the rapid, the deeper the powerful undercurrent. The top of the water feels like silken glass, and underneath, torrents surge, rumbling along the riverbed. It's the most magnificent feeling to connect to the deep, raging undercurrent and, at the same time, feel the bottom of my boat floating on the smooth satin, iridescent water.

Once in a while, as I put my oar in the river at the V's beginning point, the glistening water, the oar, my hand, body, river, and boat are all one: one unit, one being, one movement.

Time stands still.

There is an infinite opportunity to lift my oar and maneuver the boat. Each move is perfection and grace. There is no separate I; everything merges as one.

The gift of facing fear and building courage is a journey into a magical realm where we are all connected. This transcendent moment ripples out as everyone experiences this opening of space-time, the union of different levels of reality, and the connection to the flow of all that is.

At the bottom of the rapids, passengers and people viewing from shore all say, "What happened?" Everyone experienced the expansive moment, where time stood still.

THE GRAND ADVENTURE
1976

Six months ago, trekking in remote regions of Nepal, I imagined myself rowing the Grand Canyon. My dreams sparkled through the valleys like prayer flags billowing in the wind. At the end of my first summer on the river, there's no glimmer of hope for me to row to the Grand Canyon.

Boating season has ended, and Roger and I, by chance, stop by the boathouse. Tired and wet, Roger's just taught me how to roll a kayak. George arrives in search of two boatmen to head to the Grand Canyon; of course, we jump at the chance. We need to leave immediately, a thirteen-hour trip, driving about 835 miles from Angels Camp, California, to Lees Ferry, Arizona.

A family of four is attempting to row a homemade rig down the Grand Canyon; they need professional guides. Amy arrives from Colorado, Roger and I drive all night from California, and Bill is already at Lees Ferry. Bill rows the wife in one raft, the husband and two boys in their makeshift boat, and Roger kayaks. Amy and I share a boat; we are some of the first women to row a rubber raft down the Grand.

To become certified to row passengers on the Grand, we need to make three trips down the river and row every rapid. This is a luxurious twenty-three-day private trip; it is rare to have that much time in the canyon. We will row 297 luscious, adventurous miles, from Lees Ferry to Lake Mead, which is about twenty miles from Las Vegas, Nevada.

The Colorado River etched its course through the canyon at least seventeen million years ago. The canyon walls soar up over a mile, exposing layers of geological history. The majestic beauty and awesome rapids make this one of the world's greatest rivers.

The rapids change daily depending on how much water is released from Glen Canyon Dam. Before every big rapid, we tie up our boats and scout the river to see how we can come out alive without flipping the boat. At mile 17.1, upstream from House Rock, the second-largest rapid on the Grand, we confer on the best possible route.

The path is clear; head in on the right, put my oar in just below the boulder. Crank a hard left, turn my boat, ferry across right as fast as possible, and turn a hard right. Then row like hell with all my might to the right, navigating between the gargantuan keeper hole and the boulder's sharp stone wall.

Keeper holes are enormous vortexes of water large enough to suck down an entire boat, passengers, and gear. The river has you in her grip, and she's not letting go. If you leave your life jacket on and try to fight your way to the top, you will drown. The only way out is to take off your life jacket, dive down into the center of the spinning vortex, down to the bottom of the river, and escape downriver.

Back in the boat, fear rises; on my right is a sheer, hard 32-foot-high granite wall; on the left is a razor-sharp rock the size of a house. In between is a narrow, thundering shoot barely wide enough to propel my boat through. At the bottom, a keeper hole.

The river thunders, swirling water vortexes greater than I've ever seen, my stomach churns, my heart pounds, and fear mounts. Careening through white-water, I misjudge the currents. My boat rides the wrong part of the wave. My left arm is shoulder-deep in the freezing river, my right oar flailing around in the sky, the boat is riding on its side, the whole bottom exposed. Will we flip?

Amy screams, "Row like a son-of-a-bitch," as she lunges to the high side of the boat. I hurl my entire body against the left oar; the oar's momentum corrects the boat mid-rapid. My boat safely slides beside the edge of the keeper hole to my left.

White flowers open that only bloom during a full moon, and light reverberates through the canyon walls. Beams of moonlight glisten on the rippling water, and luscious fragrance swirls as a warm breeze travels upriver. It's impossible to sleep. Magic sparkles sprinkle the river and the sandy beach. Senses heightened, alchemy fills the air. Even the sound of the river feels saturated with divine pleasure.

Twenty-three days in the canyon is a fantastic gift. A new level of attunement to nature takes place. My body synchronizes with the river's ebb and flow, the moonlight cycle, and the rhythms of nature.

Each day, more spectacular than the last, the teenage boys eat more than planned. At the end of the trip, we had one can of tomato soup left, that's it.

At summer's end, coming off the Grand, looking in a mirror, I am shocked to see my muscles, my river-worn, wrinkled skin, and the deep calluses on my hands. After my first hot shower in what feels like an eternity, I dig a semi-clean long-sleeved blouse out of the bottom of my sandy rubber black bag. When I lift my arms to brush my hair, my bulging biceps rip the sleeves of my blouse. It's not cool to be fit and muscular; in 1976, women were expected to be helpless, docile, and subservient.

After six months of living under the stars, I was exhausted the first night I slept inside. I spent the night trying to row my bed/boat out the window.

Eleven boatmen converge, arriving from the country's wildest rivers, and descend on our yellow school bus to outfit it for a trip to Alaska. The white-water rafting season just ended on the Rogue River in Oregon. For the next few hours, boatmen crawl all over two buses, transferring gear from one bus to another. The guys remove the back few rows of seats to hold equipment and food for the professional trips. Boats, bright orange life jackets, and oars soar to the roof. A fabulous sound system was installed; the Beatles, "Here Comes the Sun," bellows through the windows.

I've heard the stories and been dreaming of Alaska for years. I drive to the nearest payphone, jam in a fistful of quarters, call my boss, and ask if I can join the other boatmen. In exchange for passage to Alaska, I offer to drive the first shuttle for free. The answer is yes.

I gather up my Rogue's season's earnings of $28 a day, stuff some clothes in a duffle bag, find a place to leave my car, and an hour later board the Magical Yellow Bus headed north. In Seattle, we shop at REI to buy clothes and mosquito repellent. Popcorn in hand, legs stretched out, twelve boatmen line the movie theater's front row and watch the first Star Wars. "May the Force be with us" becomes our motto.

The Alaska Ferry buzzes with the sight of twelve scruffy, tan, water-worn boatmen. We are the talk of the ferry passengers. Some people are smiling, others with looks of disbelief, disdain, or utter disapproval. Looked at with a wary eye, little did we know we were fashion trendsetters. Muscular, toned bodies, sun-streaked hair, T-shirts, cut-offs, ripped jeans, tennis shoes, and expensive polarized dark glasses. We were just fifty years ahead of our time. Today, people pay a small fortune to emulate our look. Our clear eyes and carved bodies exude confidence and a core connection to nature's wildness.

We pitch three prototypes of the first dome tents on the ferry's top deck. People have never seen a tent that stood up on its own before. Dome tents plopped down on the upper deck appear to have arrived from outer space. Below deck, "Lucy in the Sky with Diamonds" blasts out the yellow magic bus.

After landing in Haines, we camped for two nights under a huge tree filled with forty or fifty bald eagles. I ask the eagles for a feather. A great eagle circles overhead, and a perfect, long feather floats down to my feet.

On the first shuttle, after dropping off the boatmen, passengers, and gear, I drive the bus up the winding, tricky road to the Alcan Highway alone. Mountains soar, beckoning me to explore. I camp for a few days under high mountain peaks near a spectacular icy-blue glacial-fed lake in the wilds.

Heading towards Haines, a car screeches at a rest stop on the Alcan Highway; the family jumps out, kids screaming, "There's the Magic Yellow Bus we saw on the ferry." I invite them in. Speakers mounted in the front and back of the bus create an all-around sound. "All You Need is Love" fills the space. The kid's eyes expand when they see the back of the bus; the last six rows of seats on both sides are missing, now almost empty, used to haul food and gear from Oregon.

Running and hopping, the kids lift themselves on rails behind both sides' seats, briefly airborne, swinging their legs forward. They venture to the back, dance, and play amongst the bright orange life vests, a few empty black rubber bags used to hold passengers' clothing, and large, empty ammo cans.

Glenda's homestead is nestled in the boonies, totally off the grid, with no running water and complete quiet. Glenda and I recognized each other on the ferry. We both used to live in Berkeley, CA, and she invited me to stay with her family in their log cabin on the outskirts of Haines.

Alongside the wood-framed rustic house is a large greenhouse to grow food and enough pot to store for the winter. On the other side of the summer garden is a sauna for the weekly family cleanse. The house has a heavy cast-iron wood-burning stove, handmade furniture, and thick rugs. A fur-covered toilet seat hangs near the back door for the freeze-your-ass-off winter treks to the outhouse.

Fresh-caught grilled salmon and just-picked blackberries crafted into pies appear as the house fills with people. The locals arrive for a party, bringing the most delicious food I've ever tasted. Live heart-pounding, body-rocking music reverberates through the landscape. When the generator runs out, people siphon gas out of their cars to keep the music flowing.

Glory colors illuminate the starry sky on the balcony of the unfinished second story. A crescent moon hangs above a river's silver ribbon; the sky is streaked with iridescent pinks, blues, and purples of the northern lights. Here on the balcony, I meet Doug, an attorney from Manhattan. We marvel at the incredible beauty.

Downstairs, I meet his friends, Joe, the Haines doctor, and Peggy, the owner of the local pizza parlor. Joe and Doug, buddies from Yale, have black labs from the same litter. In this magical moment, we all decide to take a river trip down the Alsek and Tatshenshini rivers, known as the Tat.

In 1977, few people had ventured down this 160-mile river that runs from Dalton Post, Canada, to Dry Bay, Alaska. A woman rowing a single boat, with no other boatmen, is a novelty.

Four people, two dogs, and two rifles loaded in one boat head out into the untouched Alaskan wilderness. This is my first trip down the Tat. I've heard stories about the sand waves and eddy lines, but that is different from real-life experience. At put-in, I watch a grizzly bear saunter into the river, scoop up a salmon in its paw, hold the flailing salmon in its mouth, and meander away. Later, checking out his tracks, I easily fit both my feet in one paw print. I'm excited, intimidated, terrified, and a bit nervous about rowing this river.

In the Tatshenshini Gorge, I row a fabulous section of perfectly formed sand waves made up of glacial silt. It is so yummy to ride the delicious curving waves that continue long after most rivers peter out. At the bottom of the rapids, the boat scrapes over an unseen sharp boulder. The river carries a glacial sludge level that makes it impossible to see an inch below the surface. I pull to shore and analyze the eighteen-inch gash in the bottom of my boat. I now fully realize why it is inadvisable to take a single boat down the Tat's remote regions.

The well-known rhythm of sewing helps ease my mounting fear about the severity of our situation. Mosquitoes, the size of flies, swarm biting everywhere. My mind races through the worst-case scenarios if the mend doesn't hold. Sewing the waxed thread in and out, I go through a mental checklist. We are near an open patch of sandy beach. We have plenty of food. One of the passengers is a doctor. After eight days, the bush pilot will miss us at takeout and search for us. We can build a smoky fire, and I can signal with the mirror in my ammo can. I don't want the others to know the depth of my inner panic. I meticulously sew, patch, and duct tape the boat; this patch has to hold.

We camp on a sandbar with views of hanging glaciers dripping off high mountain peaks. We are rafting through twenty-seven million acres of nature preserves, the world's largest contiguous wilderness area. The mythic proportions of the landscape intensify my feelings of vulnerability. Clusters of flaming fireweed and purple lupine, along with a vast array of animal tracks, blanket our campsite. We are tender morsels to the mammals roaming these parts. The dogs sleep in the tents with us; the guys sleep with rifles nearby.

Over the next days, the valley continues to open while extensive tributaries pour into the Tat, transforming it into an immense river. Silt, sand, and glacial debris create channels in the river that snag the boat. A panorama of sweeping, awe-inspiring vistas surrounds us. Fluttering birds' wings, bald eagles screech, scurrying animals, breaking twigs, howling wolves, and the deep sandpaper sound of rumbling glacial silt etching the bottom of the boat are engulfed in the massive silence of vast, untouched space.

Ever since my spontaneous Kundalini awakening, I've been aware that everything is consciousness. We are in real nature, untouched by human hands. There are no human thought waves imprinted in the surroundings; nothing stamped with the consciousness of humanity. I row free of the old paradigm's human choking patterns that shut down my brain waves and nervous system. To touch this pristine ground is such an exquisite, rare privilege.

At the confluence of the Tatshenshini and Alsek, the size and hydraulics of the river are impressive. The river swells to over a mile wide. Ribbons of woven glacial sludge create mid-stream sandbars. Eddy lines stand tall. An eddy is a swirling of water in the opposite direction of the main flow of a river. A sheer line divides the slower water spinning upstream apart from the downstream current. The zone between the screaming downstream flow and the upstream spin creates eddy lines several feet high on the Tat's formidable water. I'd heard about these, but I gasped when I encountered the hydraulics of this river.

Take a moment and put your elbow on a table. Point your fingers to the sky and measure twenty-four inches up from your elbow. Imagine that the table is water forcefully flowing upstream. The mark two feet up is water churning downstream in the opposite direction. Like your arm, A straight wall of water stands between the two water levels. That is what the eddy lines or eddy fences are like on the Tat.

On day six, after camping on a glacial moraine, we secure the gear and gather up the dogs. Out of the blue, a massive grizzly pulls up to shore. Grizzly bears move at a speed of twenty-seven to thirty-five miles an hour. Panic sets in; there is no way I can out-row a grizzly. The guys dig for the guns, Peggy grabs the dogs, and I row for dear life. Interwoven sandbars catch the boat. The grizzly stands up on his hind feet, raises his paws to the sky, exposing a nine-foot frame, and lets out a husky roar that reverberates throughout the wilderness. He turns and strolls, disappearing into the backcountry. It was then that I learned that grizzly bears don't like dogs.

Still shaking, I row as fast as possible. Low-hung clouds blank out the mountains. The arctic chill clamors up our legs. An eagle dips into a close-up view as if it is checking us out. The braided river keeps snagging the boat. Huge eddy lines appear and disappear as we float by. Moose grazing close to the shore look up and track our lone boat drifting through the vast, untouched expanse. The frigid air is somber and pensive—a wolf howls.

The next day snow capped 15,300' regal Mount Fairweather crowns the St. Elias Mountains, the largest concentration of high peaks in North America. An iceberg the size of an ocean liner blocks one of the entrances to Lake Alsek. I find a pathway through the ever-shifting icebergs. Massive curving glaciers spill into Alsek Lake. The calving glaciers thunder as vast chunks of ice, the size of large buildings, plunge into the lake—the ice crackles, like the sound of pouring hot water on a tray of ice, only more deep-rooted and ricochets through the icebergs.

I weave my way through the largest non-polar ice field in the world. To my right, an iceberg flips over, creating rippling waves that rock the boat. Mysterious shapes of ice radiate a chilling, luminous blue light. Gargantuan holes, twisted shapes, and rounded contours etched in the icebergs testify to the howling winds that whip through this valley.

After eight days on the river, we landed at the fishery in Dry Bay. The next morning, a bush pilot flies in, loads our gear, and we have a spectacular flight over the rugged, magnificent country back to Haines.

I'm one of the lucky ones; I lived in the wilderness for five years—no tent to offer a sense of security, just a sleeping bag. Alone, open, vulnerable, held in nature's arms, drenched in moonlight, the entire cosmos looks over me and keeps me safe and protected.

I merge more deeply with nature. Wild nature is my real home, a place where I am safe. I trust wild animals way more than any human I've ever known.

My home comprises two black neoprene bags, the river, and the sky for five lusciously long river seasons. One black bag holds my sleeping bag and ground cloth. The blue rectangular ground cloth goes under my 1/4" insolite pad when the ground is wet or damp. When it rains, it becomes a lean-to shelter, and when the sand blows upriver at night, I wrap the crunchy cloth around my sleeping bag and head.

The trick is to sit on the black bag to get all the air out so both the sleeping bag and ground cloth fit, quickly roll the top down enough turns to make an airtight seal, and then thread the tabs into buckles on each side of the bag to keep the water out. The other black bag holds a long dress, a kimono, two blouses, a towel, a bathing suit, rain pants, a jacket, scarves, and a hat. Torn cut-offs and ripped jeans, not the expensive ones found today, but ragged from use. Everything smells like an old rubber tire and has slightly damp sandy grit.

I have the fantastic opportunity to row the Stanislaus, American, Middle Fork of the Salmon, Rogue, Grand Canyon, Cataract Canyon, Green, Alsek and Tatshenshini, West Water, Dolores, Roaring Fork, and the first exploratory trip down the Copper River in Alaska.

I witnessed people's lives change. I've heard from passengers who switched jobs and careers, shifted their lives, and had a new outlook on life due to the transformation that took place on the river.

The river is my escape into a magical reality. My body relaxes, the inner panic subsides, and the pain lessens. Daily, I face the fear of the rapids, which brings solace to my inner demons. My childhood environment from conception was one of fear, terror, and annihilation. I unwind, take a deep breath, and release the heavy armor protecting my vulnerability.

On the river, I see the terror in front of me, right before my eyes. The fear isn't hidden in the recesses of my unconscious, deeply buried in memories, silenced in my throat, or encoded in my DNA. The clear water of the river mixed with clean, fresh air and sunlight adds significantly to my well-being. The remote canyons are free from electromagnetic TV and radio waves and alternating currents of electricity.

My body comes to more and more peace. The pain slowly subsides, and the recurring nightmares melt into remission. I feel at home on the river; my heart opens. The sacred medicine of my love for the river was revealed.

For five years, I worked as one of the first female white water river guides. Reflecting, I think those were my happiest years. I had the time of my life, hurling rubber rafts down raging rivers with rapids big enough to eat my boat and kill all of my passengers. It's time to move on, satiated with the tantalizing feast of the river. Hot bubble baths, clean, smooth sheets, a soft bed, a comfy couch, and new stimulation for my mind beckoned me back to the world. The Shakti surging through my body pushes me forward to the next adventure of this life.

The river is my greatest teacher, revealing her secrets while my inner seeing expands. My years as a professional white-water guide come to a close, opening the door for a different type of journey.

MOONLIGHT ASCENT OF MT. SOPRIS
1980

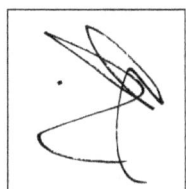

Like a wounded animal, when the pain becomes unbearable, I seek refuge in the comfort of the lone wilderness. I escape into nature to find myself, my essence. The wild backcountry keeps me alive, not the grazed pastures of a ranch or the tamed grasses of a golf course. I devour the savage vistas of jagged mountains, high alpine meadows, untouched forests, and free-running rivers. I love real nature, not the out-of-doors sculpted and molded by man.

Nature's wildness soothes my soul as I explore deeper into the unknown, as far away from mankind as possible. The word mankind is such an oxymoron. What is kind about men who destroy the Earth, rape, and kill for power and greed? My goal is to distance myself from the craziness, violence, and brutality of people. I trust nature and wild animals; I don't trust people and animals influenced by man.

Each solo adventure is progressively more challenging. I push and test my boundaries. Am I connected with nature deep enough to survive? Do I know how to tune in with the wild animals to camp unprotected in the darkness with safety?

Over the years, my solo wilderness treks became more extreme. I arrange my work schedule so no one will miss me, even if I'm gone for a few extra days. I never tell anyone where I'm going. I don't sign the Forest Service register. I always enter the wilds miles away from where I park my car. I never follow a trail; I only travel through the unmarked wilderness. If I see or hear people, I hide so they don't see me. I only use a tent if it's winter and snowing.

On each outing, I up my survival tests. On this adventure, I add to the list - no map, no compass, no mirror (to signal for help), and no flashlight. Can I make it out in one piece, unscathed? If I don't survive, that's fine. Weapons-grade radiation, designed to annihilate, rips through my body. The pain is so intense; I'm living on the edge, dancing between wanting to live or die. The inner voice of annihilation whispers throughout my cells, like a siren pulling me into the wilds.

This solo is a moonlight climb of Mt. Sopris down the valley from Aspen, Colorado, where I live. Part of the Elk Range, Mt. Sopris boasts unusual colors, milky light gray coarse-grained granite boulders, and purplish-red crumbling sedimentary rocks.

I broke one of my main rules after trekking through the backcountry for a few miles. I hear someone crying. The sobs guide me to a terrified little girl clutching her knees, rocking back and forth in a field of wildflowers. She is part of a Girl Scout Troop overnight campout. She meandered away from the group, panicked, and kept moving further into the unknown. After comforting her, the girl and I set out to find her group.

Chaos runs rampant at the Girl Scouts' campsite. Mismatched poles poke out of the wrong tent loops, tent flies are backward, and haphazard cooking gear covers the splintered wood picnic table. Girl Scouts wander around in confusion. When we arrive, the leader brushes the girl aside. Never missed in the turmoil, she slumps down on the picnic table bench.

Again, I leave the trail, find a place to stash my backpack, and make mental notes of nature's signposts so I can find my pack after my ascent of Mt. Sopris.

My progress is slow. Sharp jagged granite slabs the size of chairs teeter in a delicate balance. Massive fallen trees interspersed with erratic shifting boulders—no stable footing. I'm sure there is a trail around the rubble at the edge of the forest, but I'm too stubborn to take the easy route.

Darkness descends while I inch my way up the slope. I press onward, creeping towards the scree slope leading up to the first false summit on the East Ridge of Mt. Sopris.

Cold wind crashes down the mountain, merging with the warmth rising from the valley. A swirling gust envelops my body, signaling a dramatic change in the weather. Ominous clouds block the moonlight. My plan to reach the summit was dashed. The gloom expands, the wind whips, and a chill runs up my spine. It is time to descend the mountain.

I stand and glance up at the sky. Voluptuous, dark rain clouds block out the full moon. An altered state envelops my consciousness, and instead of taking a step, I leap. The Earth relaxes her gravity grip. I become light. I bound up in an arc and landed ten to fifteen feet down the rough slope. I glide over slippery boulders, pointed edges, and tipping rocks. Every step vaults over giant fallen trees, sharp jagged granite rocks, and I barely touch the ground from one upsurge to the next.

What the hell am I doing? Thoughts creep into my left brain. What if I fall and break my leg? This is twisted-ankle, leg-breaking terrain. I could be up here for days before anyone would even miss me. The fear of serious trouble takes over. I stop, sit down, and breathe deeply. Fear slides down my body and out of my feet; in exchange, the Earth fills me with safety and love. My heart opens, drinking in unfettered wildness.

Relaxed, I rise and search for the moon. Within seconds, my right brain shifts into an altered state, I take a step, or rather a hop, into space, transformed into another time and place, into another dimension. Leaping, soaring, flying down the slope, jumping over jagged, craggy edges, and sharp, broken branches, I glide lightly touching the Earth, bounding down the mountain. My feet almost rebound from one jagged, unstable rock to the next, prancing in a distinct rhythm. Tipsy boulders, drunk on nature's elixir, teeter on the brink of collapse. Razor-sharp rocks slice the darkness.

What if I gash my leg on a sharp rock? How will I ever find my backpack in the dark? Again, my reptilian brain fear creeps in and cascades through my body. I stop, sit, and talk to myself. Just slide your butt along the rocks, and eventually, you'll be off the slope. You're wearing your old jeans; it doesn't matter if they rip.

Alexandra David-Neel's book about Tibet comes to mind. Of the thirty-five books I devoured before leaving for Nepal, one part of her book always stood out: Tibetan monks leaping across the Tibetan plateau. Reading her words, I wanted the visceral experience of jumping through space. So, that's what is happening; I'm lung-gom-pa running.

The clouds intensify. I gaze up, and a small, radiant line exposes the edge of the moon. Again, I shift into an altered state, transported beyond third-dimensional reality into another world known in the past but blurred out in the present. Instinctively, I keep my focus on the luminous edge. I rise and soar, touching down on unstable rocks and round tree trunks with branches poking out. I am free, unshackled, gliding down the mountain with ease and grace. And then I come to an abrupt halt. I turn left and walk deep into the woods, and again come to a stop. To my right, my backpack rests next to a tree.

In the black night, I never would have been able to find my backpack. All the markings in nature I so carefully studied were obliterated in the darkness. An inner sense took over, directing me. That night, under the protection of my tarp, hitched to two trees, I dreamt of far-off places and magical lands.

Safely back home, I reread *Magic and Mystery in Tibet*. In 1924, Alexandra David-Neel was the first European woman to reach Lhasa, Tibet's remote and forbidden capital. She was also the first, and perhaps only, Westerner to observe a running *lung-gom-pa*. David-Neel wrote, "By the time he had nearly reached us, I could clearly see his perfectly calm, impassive face and wide-open eyes with their gaze fixed on some invisible far-distant object situated somewhere high up in space. The man did not run. He seemed to lift himself from the ground, proceeding by leaps. It looked as if he had been endowed with the elasticity of a ball and rebounded each time his feet touched the ground. His steps had the regularity of a pendulum."

The *lung-gom-pa* runners of old Tibet are similar to the Marathon monks of Japan. After years of intense meditation practices, they can fly like the wind. During their runs, they continually fix their gaze on a star. My Google search revealed they travel nonstop for forty-eight hours or more and can cover more than 200 miles a day.

According to some schools of thought, I jumped timelines. All timelines exist in the now, superimposed on each other like a hologram. Different ways of understanding might say I am connected to a past life. Or, the channel Abraham-Hicks talks about shooting out rockets of desire, which then manifest. Perhaps my desire was so strong that the whole experience started into motion back when I read the book. I'm not sure which explanation is accurate, and I'm sure there are many other viewpoints to consider.

From my perspective, ancient memories were activated that night. I experienced another time and reality, a dimension encoded in my DNA connected to my inner seeing.

PH.D. CELLULAR TRANSFORMATION
1982 - 85

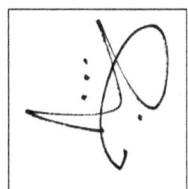

I want answers.

It's been eight years since the crisp November day in 1974 when my spontaneous Kundalini awakening occurred. As more bizarre experiences happened, I decided to explore that split second, from one breath to the next, when my consciousness exploded into multiple dimensions. I have no framework to hold my experiences, dimensions of seeing, and my inner knowing. The main impetus to receive my Ph.D. is to understand and communicate the magical things taking place. My ability to see into the subatomic particles of nature taught me quantum physics. How do I take the river's mysteries and my inner seeing and translate that into concrete 3-D language that others will understand?

From one breath to the next, the Sushumna's central channel opened fully during my spontaneous Kundalini awakening. Shakti, the serpent power of awakening and evolution, now flows like a great river, from the base of my spine to my brain, igniting new neural connections of my cosmic multidimensional inner seeing and sensing.

At times, I'm on fire, throbbing energy surges, clearing out the two channels that start near my root, weave back and forth like snakes, and converge at the top of my head. The two channels, known as Ida and Pingala, look like the double helix of DNA, or the caduceus, the symbol of modern medicine. There's no escaping Shakti's all-consuming, fiery pounding energy that burns up the channels. The force is so strong that she eats the debris in her path. The raging rapids of the wildest rivers match the power of Shakti surging through my body.

Shakti also takes a different route that's not in the books I've read. She meanders down my legs and seeps from her triangular pocket at the base of my spine. She exudes her delicious nectar throughout my body, cells drink in her divine elixir, shifting my reality.

Shakti's power, awakening, and force helped me connect with the river in profound ways. How do I take this knowledge and translate it into a doctoral dissertation?

Weaving together the puzzle of my life with scientific research becomes an exciting adventure. Every night in my dream state, I visit an enchanted place and meet my friends. We relax on exquisite carpets during these nocturnal visits, floating on a cloud, traveling through the cosmos. A soft mist surrounds the group, obscuring faces. These are my teachers and my equals. The dialogue is non-verbal. Each night we consider different sciences and topics, venturing beyond the space/time continuum, laughing and sipping tea from gold-rimmed cups.

Instead of seeing a glorious, exquisite rug, I open my eyes to a worn, nondescript beige carpet every morning, the path to the door worn flat. With a jolt, I am back on Earth for the day.

In the library, books fall off the shelves. Sometimes books poke out of the stacks, calling me. Titles lift off the cover of other books. I check the books out and go home to read and study. During the day, I write and research what I receive in the night. I probe a plethora of sciences. I have no idea what I am studying or what my thesis is about for the first year. I made up something to tell the graduate school, but I don't have a clue. The nightly visits and daily work continue for three years.

My ideas and theories are so far out that I need scientific backing.

Cosmic Inner Seeing

Whenever I speak about what I know and see, people treat me like a flake, a stupid woman, or an airy-fairy hippie. To explain what I observe and know in my guts, I use multiple disciplines to squish my wisdom into the tiny boxes of the old paradigm.

I start by bridging the gap between my inner knowing and logic; I invite the neural pathways to connect between the right and left hemispheres of my brain, like wormholes from one reality to another. Tiny neurons burrow their way through the corpus callosum, a broad, thick, arched bridge of tissue that connects the two cerebral hemispheres, allowing communication between the right and left sides of my brain.

I want to bring words into what I see and what I know. I invite left-brain neurons connected to my language centers to take an unknown journey through the corpus callosum into my right brain and down into my cells. Slightly painful, it feels like excavating a tunnel through dense matter. I learn the language of the cells.

I also explore the languages of quantum physics, metaphysics, psychology, molecular biology, shamanism, healing arts, Shakti, Kundalini, spirituality, philosophy, and systems theory. I sink my teeth into, chew on, digest, and assimilate each different language. How does the nature of the cosmos relate to the knowledge encoded in DNA? How do the laws of quantum physics inform cellular alchemy?

Before the computer age and Google, I typed up copious notes and printed them out. Each of the 212 books I studied has a different configuration of colors, drawn down every page of notes. That way, when I cut the sheets into strips, I'll know which book to quote.

What are the common threads of these language systems saying? Chaos ensues; scraps of paper fly across the living room floor. Bit by bit, each shred joins others, saying something similar. I end up with seven piles of notes and quotes. I weave these threads together, revealing the vision of my thesis.

Seven stages of change, repeated throughout nature and different sciences, confirm the cycles that comprise life. Until the blocks at the cellular level are removed and the subconscious and unconscious patterns transformed, we keep re-experiencing the same old structure of reality.

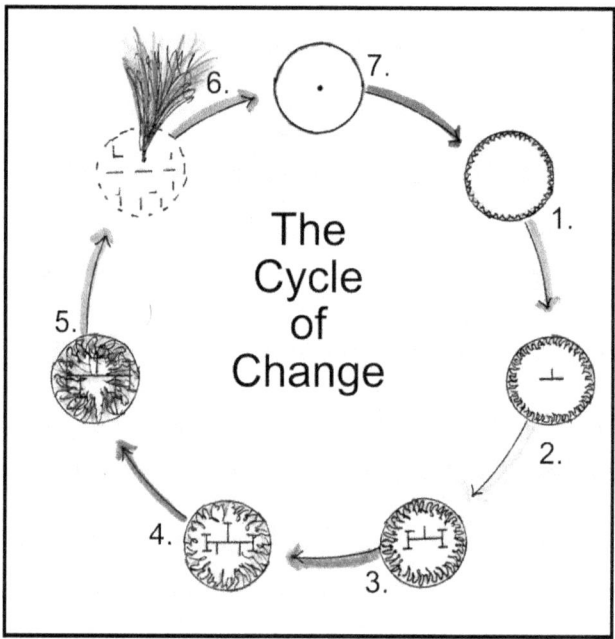

1. Pain or Pleasure - A catalyst, either internal or external, propels us into the new.

2. New Idea - As the pain or creative movement towards something different builds, a new idea is introduced.

3. Groundwork - This is the beginning of an in-between state, gathering information, and fact-finding.

4. Incubation - The incubation period can be a time of frustration due to the outward appearance of a lack of significant change. The change is internal.

5. Critical Mass - At the point of critical mass, the new replaces the old structure. During this process, there is the experience of death, darkness, despair, and or depression. The old is experienced for the final time as it leaves the body.

6. Breakthrough - The old structure of reality dissolves into a new

arrangement of reality. Changes in nature are explosive, not continuous, and smooth.

7. Actualization - After the breakthrough stage, we experience living in the new structure of reality. We are actualizing the universe.

Consciousness is everywhere, a net of unseen connections in the multidimensional quantum field. Transforming the underlying circuitry or neurological structure, all the way down to the DNA, profound change occurs, rippling out into every aspect of a person's life and throughout the world. By deliberately shifting our cellular structures, we can alter our reality in far-reaching ways.

Our inherited and childhood circuitry is filled with toxins and junk unrelated to who we are. Squished into an internal structure, passed down for generations, hides the essence of who we are. As the old is cleared, there is more space for the soul essence to shine through.

The two words together, cellular and transformation, were a new combination in 1985. Even though my Ph.D. is in psychology, my thesis relies heavily on the quantum physics I learned from the river. I received my doctorate in the Psychology of Change and Cellular Transformation and am a pioneer in this field; getting my degree changed everything.

The way to transform the world is to change our DNA.

HEALING ANGELS
1985

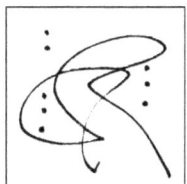

New Ph.D. in hand, I take a risk. I have one client referral in a city where I know no one. Filled with trepidation, excitement, and hope, I load up a U-Haul van, attach a tow bar for my car, and drive to Montana.

Light streams in the window, and crystals sparkle colors throughout my office. Next to a teak desk, my chair faces a plush velvet recliner for my client to relax and feel safe. I'm the first female Ph.D. psychotherapist in Billings. It's 1985; I'm thirty-nine.

Iridescent angelic energy swirls through my office. Angels appear in many cultures and religions around the world. Unlike the angelic hierarchy connected to religious beliefs, I work with a group of celestial beings, dedicated to healing humanity, that I've known my whole life.

Minuscule angels dance around particles inside cells, cleaning up residue on sub-atomic levels. Angel wings flutter, clearing old debris. Celestial frequencies dismantle ancient, harmful, dysfunctional programs. Wings vary from radiant colors, something like feathers, to billowy clouds. The shapes can be round, little fairy wings, or enormous arched wings flowing to the ground. Some angels are large enough to surround the Earth with their magnificent, majestic wings.

Waiting in the wings, when invited, angels delight in being of service to humanity's evolution.

After my office opening announcing my new private practice, the good old boys' network joins forces and tries to run me out of town. Not wanting a woman invading their territory, they send their top dog therapist to take me to lunch. I arrive in a soft light grey fitted jacket, silk blouse, above-the-knee-length skirt, stockings, heels, and pearls. I'm used to conducting business meetings in beautiful upscale restaurants, with exquisite table settings and delicious food. I was shocked to meet Dr. Robertson at a greasy dive. White Formica-top tables, crumpled paper napkins jammed in a plastic holder, metal chairs with tacky red synthetic leather seats. The menu, a gummy laminated sheet of paper, breakfast on one side, lunch on the other - macaroni and cheese, hamburgers, and grilled cheese sandwiches are the lunch choices.

Dr. Robertson turns on his white male supremacy intimidation tactics and tells me the other male therapists in town won't refer clients to me. I learned they intend to blackball me from the Montana Psychological Association. I'm thankful for the information. Much to his surprise, I picked up the lunch tab.

In retrospect, the good old boys' rejecting me was a gift. I discovered how to use my inner seeing without the external constraints of fitting into the male paradigm. My work took on its own trajectory, which continues to this day.

Women flock to my office. One woman burst into tears when she saw the peach blush walls and cozy velvet couch with soft pillows. "Oh, thank goodness, I can breathe," were the first words out of her mouth.

When I met Emily, she could barely walk. Her toes curled up under her feet. Surgeons cut the back of every toe to straighten them out enough so she could walk. The surgery was successful for a few years, and then her toes bound up again. After a few operations on each toe, she came to me.

Have you ever looked inside a golf ball and seen those tightly wrapped rubber bands? That is what I see inside her toes. The tiny rubber bands are thought forms, strings of words. "You'll never amount to anything. You won't stand on your own two feet. You are worthless." Her mother's comments crippled her. She took her mother's words into her body, as we all do.

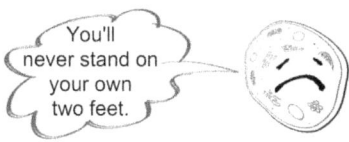

We disentangled all the negative words, thoughts, and energies snarled around each toe. It took months to unravel and free up each of Emily's toes; we accomplished something the mainstream medical profession could not touch. As we lovingly unbound Emily's toes, I had insights into the Chinese practice of foot binding and the depth of cutting off the feminine in the world. After completing our sessions, Emily was able to stand her ground, take a stance on her own two feet, and radically change her life. She moved to her own apartment, got a job, and started a relationship.

New behaviors, thoughts, and insights arise as the body clears the toxic past. Emily's case is a prime example. Surgically cutting her toes did nothing to cure her inner programs and only traumatized her body further.

Word spread quickly, and my practice flourished. Even though I never advertise, sexually abused women flock to my office. I have no specialized training, yet I know what to do.

Jackie, a twenty-six-year-old nurse, came to me in desperation. Her relationship was a mess. Every time she had sex, she ended up with a bladder infection. She went to every specialist, and the doctors had nothing for her. Jackie was at a point of hopelessness about ever having sex without pain, a relationship, a partner, or a husband. All her relationships took the same route. She felt inadequate for not being able to have sex without fear of infection. Her partner felt tormented by the internal conflict between wanting to have sex and feeling guilty for creating massive pain.

Jackie leans back in the recliner, pulls the lever to raise the footrest, and sinks into soft velvet.

"Take a deep breath and relax. Where does your body feel tight or tense?" I ask.

Trauma hides in the unconscious, beyond physical sight.

I close my eyes and journey inward, and the energy in the room shifts. The field opens; Jackie becomes aware of things previously hidden. We travel inward into other dimensions, looking for the cause of her bladder infections when she has sex.

From another dimension, what I see is similar to a rose branch with sharp thorns jammed up her vagina, poking into her bladder. There's no literal rose branch stuck up her vagina; it hasn't manifested into form, but it still energetically impacts her life.

When she was a child, her brother raped her. Her body embedded the etheric wound of incest. As an adult, with each in-and-out penis movement, invisible thorns rip through her bladder, causing inflammation and infection. The trauma deepens every time she makes love.

The healing angels surround the thorns with gobs of thick peachy-pink etheric salve to prevent shredding the tissue. A few tiny angels pull out the implant. Energetic goo and puss ooze from the wound. The angels clean the mess; we replace the damage with love and stitch it up.

Other angels sweep their wings through her uterus and vagina, healing the violated tissue. Shame, guilt, and self-hatred from being raped transform into self-acceptance and self-love. Angel wings sweep out heartbreak. Removing the barb stops the bladder infections. After months of deep inner work, Jackie opened her heart, knowing she could give and receive the full depth of love with her partner. Her life transformed. She met a man, married, and had a juicy, fulfilling sex life.

When I first met Susan, her screaming anguish and terror-filled voice was unbearable. After we completed our work together, eight of her coworkers came to see me one by one. They each said the same thing. They didn't want to know why she came to see me or anything personal about her. Susan's change was so dramatic that they wanted to meet me and say thank you.

After the rape energy cleared, Susan's frequency changed dramatically. The high frequency of her soul radiated, touching the lives of each of the mentally disabled children she worked with. The parents came to love her for the incredible changes happening in their children's lives.

I notice a pattern emerging with my clients. They each begin to see angels and other unexplainable things. They have permission and safety to explore their inner regions. They all tell me multidimensional, paranormal, unusual things they have experienced but were afraid to tell anyone else for fear of being ridiculed, made wrong, or belittled.

I paid off my small business loan in record time. One year and a week after arriving in Montana and starting my first private practice, I moved into my new home. I bought my dream house up in the mountains past Red Lodge, a passive solar house on an acre of pristine organic land. A mountain stream gurgles through my backyard.

On New Year's Day, the direction and slope of the windows capture the winter sun. Warm rays seep into the living room wall, creating a cozy, beautifully held energy. Outside it is 30° below zero, inside the house, it is a toasty 68° with no other heat than the sun. My passive solar home emits a spiraling heat, moving between the window and the heat-retaining wall, circulating nature's loving, nurturing frequency.

The eaves' slant blocks the summer sun and keeps the house cool in 100° blazing heat. My home, a safe refuge, attuned to nature, feeds and supports me on many levels and dimensions.

My closest neighbors, Nancy and John, live about a mile away. We became dear friends. Nancy, the head nurse at the largest hospital in Billings, came to me for the hardening of her arteries. Her doctor recommended an angioplasty to scrape out her closing arteries. As we worked, an angel Nancy named Madeline appeared to assist. Every day, Madeline swept her wings through Nancy's arteries, cleaning out layers of built-up toxins. After three months, she went back to her doctor. Her test results showed clear arteries. Nancy asked if the doctor wanted to know what she did; his reply was no.

The angelic energies present when working with my clients fill me with delight and joy. I discovered the book, *To Hear The Angels Sing: An Odyssey of Co-Creation With The Devic Kingdom*, by Dorothy MacLean. One of the founding members of Findhorn in Scotland, MacLean explores universal consciousness concepts by transforming sandy earth into vibrant gardens. I invite the elementals, devas, and landscape angels to guide me in my garden.

The angels, devas, and elementals show me what plants love to be around each other. It feels like having best friends over for a garden party. I sing and chant as I pick delicious, juicy, brilliant red strawberries. The river gurgles in response. The air glistens, plants smile, birds chirp. The divas, elementals, and angels play, weaving streams of love and sparkle around the backyard. Lettuce planted in the shape of an OM symbol ripples 'Let us OM' through the garden. A fire pit on the sandy strip by the river, surrounded by sage, illuminates the playful laughter of friends. Pine, sage, and mint waft on a billowing breeze, enriching the garden. The flag I made of an angel blowing a horn flutters in the gentle wind.

I welcomed the landscape angels into the backyard, but I forgot about the front yard. A few months later, a large gathering of people arrived at my home. Everyone comments on the magic and beautiful plants in the backyard, then asks me what happened to the front yard. The front yard is barren and desolate compared to the vibrant, lush, alive backyard.

Deer, bear, and other wild animals frequent my garden. Next to the river is a grassy spot dotted with wildflowers and glistening pine trees. I love deer, invite them into this magical patch, and ask the deer to stay out of the vegetable garden until invited.

One evening, at the end of the summer, I welcome the deer into the garden. The next morning, much to my delight, I woke to deer grazing on the remains of the vegetables. Tails wiggle, ears move, heads bob, munching veggies. One by one, with grace and serenity, each deer raises its head and looks me square in the eye through the picture window. I detect a glint in the eye, a nod of the head, almost a smile, acknowledging my presence.

One night, unknown celestial visitors arrive. The next morning, Nancy called to tell me about the colossal light they saw shining up from the river in my backyard. They only noticed when their dog barked, facing my house, hair standing straight up, pacing, waking them up in the night.

Curious, I bundle up in the harsh weather—glistening, sparkling, frozen particles twinkle in the crisp azure morning sky. My Sorel pac boots squeak in the pristine snow covering the thick frozen river. The weight of my body squishes the light snow crystals, leaving deep boot imprints.

Yesterday, snow concealed the thick ice of the frozen river. This morning, at the river's bend, the snow has melted in the broadest part of the river, and the ice is fragile. It's 20° below, way too cold for snow and ice to melt. Beautiful, delicate snow crystals slightly melted and then refrozen, stacked on top of each other, each about four inches high and two inches wide, create two precise circles. Perfect circles, the outer one about twelve feet in diameter; inside is a smaller sphere about ten feet across. In between the two concentric rings, small round ridges are frozen in the ice. This is where my neighbors saw the light coming up from the river last night

Near the center of the two circles, a group of stacked-up snow crystals reveals the image of an angel blowing a horn, the same image on my backyard flag.

Delighted, loved, and honored, I want to stay outside, dance, and absorb the magical presence, but it's way too cold.

Over the years, my seeing shifts. Immediately after my spontaneous awakening, I wanted to block out everything. Walking down the street was overwhelming; I saw too much. Working with clients refined my vision, seeing new ways to create profound, lasting change. I transmute neural patterns, cellular programs, and release dysfunctional sequences held in the DNA. I explore inside people's bodies to discover how transformation works.

Like my house between two gardens, I'm between two worlds: the magic of angels, mysteries, unseen forces, and the logical world of work and presenting the acceptable, correct image. In 1985, it felt scary and unsafe to come out of hiding and expose my multidimensional awareness and inner seeing.

DAD AND QUANTUM PHYSICS
1986

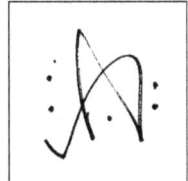

Every few years, my parents and I endure each other's company for a couple of days. At my parents' house in San Juan Capistrano, California, I find Dad reading in the den. Hanging on the wall next to his chair is a leopard skin mounted on black felt. I remember the day well, back in India in 1964. The villagers brought the leopard to Dad as a gift. It was shot while trying to flee with a young child during the famine. That day, the fur was slightly warm; rigor mortis had not set in yet.

Dad is sitting in his favorite brown leather overstuffed club chair. Once used by monks in Buddhist ceremonies, a six-foot brass Tibetan horn, now transformed into a floor lamp, lights the page. Dad is reading my doctoral dissertation. Much of my thesis, based on quantum physics, I learned from the river.

Along with my thesis, I also brought a copy of the latest National Geographic, June 1986. Men, clad in shorts and dark glasses, sit in Adirondack chairs, waiting to witness the first hydrogen bomb explosion. On page 818, I point to a man seated at the end of the third row, leaning forward in anticipation. "Is that you?" I ask Dad.

DR. CYNTHIA MILLER

National Geographic, Photo Air Force

"Ringside seats for the 'bomb' were a hot ticket in 1951, when military and civilian VIPs watched from the officers club in Eniwetok, just 12.5 miles from ground zero."

"Yes, that's me." He replies. A surge of incongruent emotions runs through my body: pride, shame, anger, fear, horror, and awe all jumbled together. Dad doesn't have great wealth, but he knows power. Watching bombs explode, destroying nature, and the erotic rush of power—these my Dad knows well.

He goes back to reading my thesis. After a few moments, he comments, "I am amazed at your depth in comprehending physics." This acknowledgment is the highest compliment I have ever received from my Dad.

I am my father's daughter; what he destroys, I discover how to transform and put back together. I inherited the underpinnings of his working knowledge of physics he used to build the world's first plutonium plant, the hydrogen bomb, and linear particle accelerators. Encoded in my DNA, a deep understanding resides, along with my dedication to the evolution of humanity's consciousness.

He goes on to say, "When I was at UCLA studying with Oppenheimer..." Dr. Robert Oppenheimer is known as the 'father of the atomic bomb.'

"Wait," I interrupt, "You studied with Oppenheimer?"

"Yes, there were four or five of us in a top-secret class studying physics with Oppenheimer."

"What was that like?" I ask.

"Well, I had trouble at times grasping some of the physics. You know, I had to take the physics and translate that into building bombs." Oppenheimer and the other physicists were brilliant; my Dad was practical; he had the genius to create nuclear warfare. Pipe smoke circles around his head; he's quiet for a time. His movements signal unspoken pain.

"Tell me more stories." I'm experiencing a rare open communication with my Dad; I want to know as much as possible. As he leans back, his reluctance to talk is evident; he has suppressed these stories for decades.

"There was the time I was on the train escorting the bombs from Los Alamos to the West Coast, headed for Japan." I knew he was talking about Little Boy and Fat Man, the bombs dropped on Hiroshima and Nagasaki in August 1945.

On the edge of the chair, I ask, "What happened?"

"I was sitting right next to the bomb, covered with a tarp. My job was to make sure nothing touched the undetonated bomb. We came to a bridge, and the trestle ripped the canvas. On the spot, I redesigned and directed the welders to change the metal structures of the bridge before we proceeded."

Reflective silence permeates the air. Smoke twists from his pipe, billowing out and filling the room with the sweet scent of tobacco. I ponder a bomb exploding on the tracks somewhere between New Mexico and California.

After a long pause, he asks, "How do you have the courage to go off alone in the wilderness? Aren't you afraid? Nature scares me." He's one of the few people on Earth who has the technical ability to destroy nature at his fingertips, yet he's terrified of nature. He knows bits and pieces of my wilderness adventures, but never the whole story.

I don't know how to reply. "No, I'm not afraid, I love nature," is my response. Decades of forced silence keep me quiet. I can't quite formulate the words of the deep terror I feel around many man-made structures, especially his, and the inner peace I feel in nature. Raw nature, as far away from people as possible, is the only place I feel safe. Nature feeds my soul and keeps me connected to my essence.

I don't speak up; undercurrents of conflict catalyze my relationship with my parents. We live in different worlds, revolving in a connected orbit with a magnetic repulsion propelling us into opposing realities.

From the living room, Mom calls, "Fix me a drink." The grimace on Dad's face upon standing signals his mounting silent agony.

In the living room, exquisite blood-red Persian carpets blanket the floor. On the Iranian brass coffee table sits the book I sent Mom for Christmas, photos of fashions I designed, made, and modeled. She's never commented on the gift. I don't know if it pisses her off, makes her feel proud, or if she's envious. Was her silence hiding her heartbreak, her unfulfilled dreams? Whatever she feels, I never hear anything positive about my creativity or my life. Was the book displayed on the coffee table just for my visit, or was she proud of her daughter?

Gulping her scotch, Mom says, "I don't know why in hell you got that damn Ph.D. Who on earth do you think you are? You should pump gas and live in your sleeping bag."

RIVER OF SOULS
1987

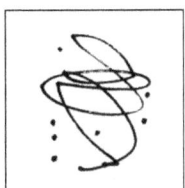

My life turns into a weird sci-fi movie, a multidimensional drama. It's mid-September 1987; I'm forty-one.

Time rewinds. I watch a massive burst of blinding white light, a fireball—vivid images of bodies vaporizing in the bombing of Hiroshima. Burning flesh drips off screaming bodies; body parts explode into nothingness- terror reigns. Toes and limbs explode into millions of tiny bits; tormented souls erupt in radioactive horror and terror. All dissolved in an instant, blasted to shreds. Buildings collapse, glass shatters, fires rage. I'm witnessing a past event, 8:15 am, August 6, 1945, the bombing of Hiroshima, Japan.

Today, I discovered why, like clockwork, I woke up screaming and ill on August 6, the anniversary of Hiroshima's bombing. Diarrhea, vomiting, sleeplessness, spiritual restlessness, high emotional anxiety, uncontrollable tears, and deep remorse occur. I am a wreck for days every year.

Time rewinds further, back to one second before the bomb. The vaporized people are whole again. And then, I watch and feel Japanese souls streaming out of my heart. I see no faces, only backs; straight, beautiful black hair, masses of people. Children in crisp white uniforms carry leather satchels of books. Years later, I discovered these same satchels in Internet photos among the ruins of Hiroshima.

Women in aprons, a few hold dish towels, grandmothers cuddle babies. Some people are half-dressed, some are naked, bathing, others comb their hair, and many are ready for work. Old men crumpled over a cane, limp, or dragged a foot. Ten across at the headwaters of my heart, they spread like a fan covering the horizon. A mass exodus of the souls of the bombing of Hiroshima has held in my heart for decades.

I'm dizzy, unsettled. Eyes open or closed, I witness souls pouring out of my wounded heart. I don't know what to do. The creek gurgles through my backyard. A Red Tail Hawk swoops over my veggie garden. Most everything happens in Billings, sixty miles away.

I'm not Catholic, but I'm pulled to see a charismatic Catholic priest in Billings. The service is in a huge high school auditorium filled with hundreds of people. After a short time, I walk down the creaky wooden bleacher steps. When the priest lays his thick, frail hands on me, his eyes bug out. He steps back and moves his head up and down, taking a good look.

He places his palms together at his chest and says, "Let's pray for the souls coming out of your heart."

Souls spill like a cloud covering the glossy, pale wood floor. We both expect the outpouring of souls to end, but they keep streaming. When the line of people waiting to see the priest grows behind me, he sends me on my way.

Still bewildered, the next day, I drove to Bozeman to stay with a friend, a master of Zen meditation. The vast stretch of road fills with Japanese, released into the wide-open countryside. Like a movie superimposed on the horizon, the Japanese fill the skyline heading towards the light rays. Vistas of blue skies, expansive space, and mountains in the distance offer freedom for the souls to journey onward. Streams of Japanese head out across the horizon, merging into infinity.

In Bozeman, my friend and I meditate and give blessings. The painful soul river flows day and night, carving open the walls of my heart, like a cervix giving birth. I can't sleep; it's hard to eat; all my life force is focused on the migrating souls.

On day three of the exodus, I met a Crow/Santee Sioux Medicine Man in Bozeman. He is about my age, long dark ponytail, barefoot, steeped in his elders' tradition. The sacred ceremonial room smells of sage. A large, thin, round drum rests on a red, beige, and brown geometric hand-woven rug. Under the window, an altar filled with sacred objects waits.

He purifies me with sage and sweetgrass. He brushes the smoke with an eagle feather as he circles the burning smudge stick around my body.

"You've come here to honor the dead?" He says

"Yes, and I would love your help," I say.

"I see souls coming out of your heart." He pauses to light more sage and incense. Souls gush out, filling the room, and follow the smoke into another dimension.

"When the white man invaded an Indian village, they killed everyone. No one was left to mourn the dead. The same thing happened in Hiroshima." The medicine man said, shaking his rattle.

"How do we mourn the dead?" I ask.

"We offer food, prayers, and songs for the journey." He places corn in the bowl on the altar next to the water.

He sings in his native tongue, beating the drum in a slow rhythm. Spirals of smoke engulf the departing souls. Rays of sunlight illuminate the altar; through the window, the Bridger Mountains sparkle in the distance.

Back at my friend's house, exhausted, I rest. Grief is intense as the outpouring continues. Little soul rivulets cascade from my toes, fingers, and bones, converge at my heart, and the souls depart. A constant stream, reaching out into infinity, as broad as my chest, spreads out across the horizon; hundreds of thousands of Japanese walk out of my heart. For five days and nights, the souls exit. Spiritual teachers from Zen, Catholic, and Native American traditions, along with the archangels and angelic hosts, are present to witness and bless the souls' evacuation. They leave, as they were one millisecond before the bomb exploded on August 6.

The most intimate form of healing possible takes place inside my heart and soul. I took on the radiation, trauma, rage, and terror of hundreds of thousands of Japanese. These are people unknown to me, who thought I was the 'enemy,' people who lived on the other side of the world. I took them all in my heart, in my body, in my cells, bones, and skin. Maybe now the pain and inner torture will subside.

Between 140,000 and 200,000 people were killed in the bombing of Hiroshima. Fragmented DNA, blown into bits, chunks of thousands of souls' DNA, needed to be mended and reunited back into the correct sequence. The bomb shattered the etheric and soul levels to bits.

As a soul keeper, my job is to weave together the shattered bits of hundreds of thousands of Japanese souls. First, I had to discover whose DNA was whose. Next, I wove together the soul fragments and DNA and connected them to their sole essence. That took over 40 years of day and night labor, fabricating them into wholeness, with a tremendous toll on my physical body. I had no idea what was happening consciously, and of course, there was no compensation, gratitude, or thanks for my years of service.

My decades of sewing, knitting, crocheting, embroidery, weaving, lacemaking, and spinning gave me the skills to patch up the blown-apart soul fragments. Imagine getting all the toes, feet, fingers, hands, arms, and heads connected to the right soul, but on a grander, more elaborate scale with all the disconnected strands and DNA bits. This process takes unending care that consumes a large part of my life's energy.

Later, I learned that the blown-up disrupted DNA of the souls would have created a massive hole in the fabric of consciousness. Not only does the use of these atomic and hydrogen weapons destroy the physical vehicles of incarnated souls, but the souls of the victims of these weapons are likewise shattered and dispersed, damaging the very fabric of the Unified Field, the Universe(s).

The magnitude of hundreds of thousands of shattered, splintered, annihilated souls, in part due to my Dad's handiwork, would cause a ripple in the cosmic net and reverberate throughout the Universe—something needed to be done to ensure the safety and continuation of the souls' existence.

The fragmented DNA needed help to connect in the correct order and sequence, shattered beyond self-repair, the soul's DNA needed physical, 3-D assistance. A job I took on, perhaps with others, and I regretted my decision for decades. I preserved the soul lineage of the Japanese bombed in Hiroshima—a tremendous lifelong cost to my health, physical, emotional, mental, and spiritual well-being. Other people took on the task of assisting the souls of Nagasaki.

Why me? Why did all those souls fill my body and pour out my heart?

CHOOSE ME
1988

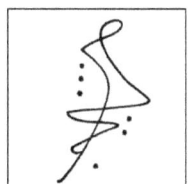

"Choose me!" I remember jumping up and down, waving my arms with enthusiasm. The space is filled with others ready to volunteer for this task. The room is solemn; the gravity in the air feels expectant and heavy. I am before the council, the board that makes the final decision on which parents one will have, and what the main path of life will be. I vehemently want this life, parents, DNA, and daunting task.

I'm in a profound otherworldly meditation; the scene takes place before my birth. In front of me is a group of radiant beings emanating light. I'm in the audience with others; we are smaller in stature than the council members before us.

The council is deliberating since the impact of what I am choosing is unknown. I'm small and inexperienced in matters of this magnitude. I don't comprehend what I'm signing up for; I just want to do it.

The world I'm headed for is at war, and new military weapons are being developed - atomic and hydrogen bombs. Humanity, a strange species, kills its own. The council deliberates further, stating that this assignment of assisting the souls killed by the first nuclear bomb was an unknown task. This task involves the evolution of consciousness for humanity. A second part, forgotten for decades, reveals itself in my later years. Some council members are reluctant, but my naive enthusiasm wins them over.

Yes, I want this task. Once embodied, I curse this choice for decades.

Over time, suppressed resentment festers. I'm pissed. Am I enslaved by the actions or karma of my father? Am I balancing my father's handiwork? Who am I serving, the lords of war, sacrifice, and poverty? The old model where the 1% become wealthy in war, and once again, I'm cleaning up their mess? The notion of renouncing myself for others is such a scam, ingrained in inherited and childhood circuitry, to keep me subservient and repressed. I've been harboring the supposed enemy in my body—an enemy filled with hatred towards me. The energy of self-hatred formed and grew inside me.

My work was unseen, unappreciated, and unpaid at such a high cost. Talk about a violation of child labor laws; I was put to work for no pay, at great detriment to my health, finances, and relationships: a fetus, the size of the tip of your finger, takes on 150,000 souls killed in the bombing of Hiroshima. I figured out that if I were paid one penny per day per soul, for forty-one years, I would be owed approximately $22,445,000. A thankless job, appreciated by few, rewarded by none.

At first, sacrificing myself feels like I'm doing an excellent service to humanity. But over the years, an inner nagging starts. Was I duped? Is crucifying myself a guise to keep the old patterns continuing? Were those Beings of Light masquerading, covering their warmongering darkness with false light? Are lightworkers helping to maintain the balance so the old paradigm can continue to function?

It takes me decades before these inner rumblings are understood and answered.

FOURTH OF JULY FIREWORKS
1989

The foul odor of rotting radioactive flesh mixed with the dirty sock smell of morphine crawls down the hall. Dad's bed is shoved into the corner of his bedroom; a hospital bed is in view. When the doctors diagnose his leukemia, the point of origin is not found, cancer spreads throughout all his bones.

"Hi, Dad."

No hello, no acknowledging my presence. Dad says, "There is a wrinkle in the sheets. Fix the damn sheets." Terror flashes in his eyes as I straighten the bottom sheet. His hands, covered with dark spots on tissue paper-thin purple skin, rest on the crisp white sheet.

Drip, slowly dripping, the morphine makes Dad angry. I've never seen him like this before. He was always calm and gentle-mannered, but now he is nasty and pissed off. He can't believe he is dying. It was nothing for him to kill hundreds of thousands of people, but he couldn't face his death. He is frightened. I wonder if he sees the faces of the Japanese being eaten with fire or smells burning flesh. Does he hear the screaming children, that bolt of fiery light consuming their tiny bodies? Weapons-grade plutonium, the frequency of annihilation, is eating him from the inside out, starting with his bones, devouring his life.

I ask, "If you could do it all over again, would you build bombs?'

"I wouldn't change a thing." The IV slowly drips morphine into his right arm; skin sags off his bones.

"The one thing I do regret is that I forced you to marry Matt." He fades off in a stupor.

Not able to move his emaciated, stinky body, he is in denial of his impending demise. He refuses to talk about death, so I write him a note asking if I can be with him when he dies. In his final moments, there might be a closure, reckoning, or even a point of coming together. His horrified response makes it very clear that he wants to perish alone.

His body is wasting away, one-half its normal size, barely able to move. "When I get out of this contraption, I'm going to play golf," he says, reflecting his terror of death.

Curled up in a ball on the bed shoved in the corner, I feel little. My Dad is dying. My relationship with my father is interwoven, not easy to unravel—so many layers from love to disrespect and disgust.

I walk to the kitchen; Mom is banging around, yelling at me, "You are such a complete failure. I have nothing to tell my friends about you." Nothing to up her status, to make others feel jealous, she is enraged that I reject her lifestyle. I am a disgrace, divorced, with a Ph.D.

Mom digs around in the back of the refrigerator and pulls out a bunch of pink and blue Tupperware containers. Moldy leftovers. She scrapes off the mold.

"A little mold never hurt anyone," she says. Dinner consists of a warmed assortment of unconnected dabs of food.

"Isn't this good?" she asks.

I am obliged to say yes; otherwise, Mom goes into temper tantrum mode. Raving about her cooking, even if untrue, is one of the few acceptable topics at dinner.

A shadow of me is present, a ghost observing. What could have been? When I was little, I loved to watch my parents dance. There was a connection; a thin thread linked their hearts. I heard stories of them dancing at the Altadena Town and Country Club and exquisite

Cosmic Inner Seeing

places. Mom is always wearing one of her latest dazzling creations, Dad is tan and fit from swimming in the South Pacific at the nuclear test site in the Bikini Islands. The crowd parted, clearing the floor. Mom and Dad glided in harmony across the polished wooden dance floor, graciously, spinning, flowing with the music. How could such dancing survive nuclear bombs, alcohol, grief, and loneliness?

What if the radiation destroyed the threads of love between my parents? All sense of family, love, joy, and delight were fried to ashes in toxic debris.

How did Mom deal with making love after not seeing him for months? I'm sure they both were ready for mad, passionate, hot, juicy sex. Her open, receptive womb receives energetically encrusted radioactive sperm spewing death and annihilation. Her sacred feminine essence was massacred. Their delicate heartstrings frayed, and brutality killed their ability to remain connected at the heart.

It all makes sense. A radioactive ball grew in her belly. She gave birth to a contaminated baby. How could she not hate me? I'm sure none of this is conscious, but her unconscious gnaws. The depth of self-hatred, self-absorption, neglect, alcohol, parties, and new clothes keeps her from collapsing in radioactive terror. Of course, she drinks. Her motto, 'Just don't think about it,' is her way to keep sane.

Dad is in his room dying, and Mom sits in her room, knitting. Clack, clack, fat royal blue yarn winds around big pink plastic knitting needles. She feels the yarn when she drops a stitch. Going blind, a detached retina in each eye, she sees a black hole surrounded by a small ring of the edge of the world.

"I don't think I needed the cancer surgery." She shows me the grisly gash in her chest. Her left breast was savagely cut off, leaving a gruesome scar on top of her heart.

Bursts of brilliant lights fill the sky—streaming rockets of golden light, radiant bursts of color, and booming sounds. On the 4th of July, 1989, Dad made his lone exit in the midst of what he loved most.

Blazing fireworks, the perfect goodbye for a man whose greatest passion and love was to watch gargantuan explosions. He was seventy-five.

My biggest adversary is gone, along with the only person I know who had a similar radiation imprint to me. I feel like I'm alone on Earth. Devastated, I cried for months. I sleep on the couch with my back wedged against the cushions. The open expanse of a bed is too vulnerable.

A complicated intertwinement still exists with Dad. This man that I loved and despised, honored and disrespected, deemed superior and inferior. This man, I felt comforted by, scared me; he violated my innermost depths.

SHAMAN'S DRUMBEAT
1989

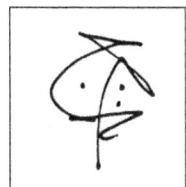

The shaman makes slow, steady drum beats; vibrations fill the room. A rattle sounding like a rattlesnake slithers around my body, opening portals into the dark past.

Again, the shaman asks if I want to take this journey. Once embarked upon, there is no way to stop or escape; I will experience the trauma fully. I say yes, I want to know what happened.

Sage smoke curls before my eyes, and the energy in the room shifts. Lying on the bed, I feel the shaman lightly touch my arm. The rhythmic drumbeat takes me deeper into another time.

The rattle hisses to a rhythmic drumbeat. I follow the heartbeat wave into my body. The journey takes me into layers hidden from consciousness, buried in my cells. The throbbing rattle and drum knock on the door to the unknown.

I see and experience myself; I'm fifteen, back at my parents' house. Passed out on the floor, screaming in pain, everyone in the house wakes up. Dr. Holder arrives in the middle of the night to shoot me up with morphine, as he has done before. The heartbeat drum continues.

I'm in bed, and my cousin-in-law comes into my room. Butch, a short, macho Marine, visits our family from time to time. His hand covers my mouth. I'm too drugged to respond. Butch takes me, robs my feminine juice, steals my divine essence for his disgusting greed. In the safety of my bed, I'm violated and disrespected.

Slowly, the drumbeat and rattle bring me back to the present.

I was fifteen when Dr. Holder shot me up with morphine. The trauma of being raped shut down my body, the morphine lodged in my cells. Now, twenty-eight years later, the locked-in morphine is set free. Morphine surges through my body.

I am too drugged to drive home; I'm too drugged to feel anything. Shut down, I'm numb.

As the morphine leaves my body, waves of anger, sadness, and tears spill, and decades of hidden shame, self-disgust, and self-hatred gush. Relief is also present, finally knowing about my nagging suspicion.

I'm shocked the morphine is so potent. I expect it to disappear in an hour; my drugged state continues for four days. At the time, I had no idea that the body held trauma in such a precise way.

I've known for years that I've been molested, I wanted to know if there was more. My Dad, covered in darkness, entered my room when I was three. The details were a blur; I was too little to comprehend what was happening. Dad came into my room in the night, his eyes black, possessed, terrifying. His head between my legs, a dark gloom enshrouded my body. In some twisted, convoluted, perverted dark ritual, my divine feminine creative essence was given up in exchange for secrets from evil forces. My innocence, the feminine energy of birth and life, was traded for information on how to build the hydrogen bomb.

I had nightmares about that for forty years. A man is chasing me; I'm running, screaming for help. During every dream, my family stood watching, ignoring me and my cries for assistance. One night, as an adult, I stopped running and faced him. The last time the dream occurred, I was chasing the man, yelling at him.

This rape, when I was a teenager, was hidden in my unconscious, yet informed my work. When I worked with sexually abused women, I knew what to say and how to proceed. One client, a beautiful fifteen-year-old girl, came to me fresh out of a drug and alcohol rehab program. A school dropout, she felt worthless and thought her only option in life was to be a prostitute. Held in a container of safety and love, we uncovered rampant rape and incest in her lineage. She had not been sexually abused, but her lineage was so infested that she carried the burden in her body. On the verge of complete self-destruction, the memory of violence was embedded in her DNA.

As one family member healed and cleared the horror and trauma, another came to my office. Over three years, eleven of her family members, all sexually abused - her mother, cousins, aunts, and even her grandmother—came to see me. We cleaned up the unspoken, hidden terror passed down in the family tree.

Sexual abuse is rampant. One-half of the women in the world will be sexually assaulted in their lifetime, most by someone she knows. This is a crisis of epic proportions. When a critical mass of sexually abused women is healed, a quantum leap for humanity will occur.

What type of global culture allows and, at times, condones this conduct towards women? What kind of sick world accepts this behavior?

Why people kill, rape, and commit violence towards each other is all connected to a more significant issue. What is the seat of this violence that permeates humanity? And, even more importantly, how can this be transmuted? What if the answers are found in DNA, hidden in another dimension?

BRIGHT RED APPLE
1990

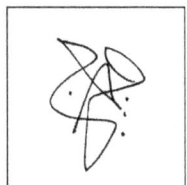

As my subconscious comes up to consciousness, bizarre events are revealed. The stuff I'm afraid to see.

Standing in the kitchen, eating a crisp, bright red apple, my stomach clenches, and the apple skin is not digesting well.

The right hemisphere of my brain says, "Remember, it always takes three days after you receive a new energetic stomach for you to digest the skin of an apple."

I remember, oh yes, it takes three days. Reflecting, last night, I was off in the healing temples with the angels, receiving a new energetic stomach. Of course, it all makes sense.

The only problem is that my logical left brain and fear-based amygdala overheard the conversation. "What the fuck, I'm getting transplants?"

My right brain responds, "That's why you're still alive; you've been getting them your whole life." I take another bite, without the apple skin.

I search through the mental files of my childhood, flying with the healing angels. Yes, they were all those nights when I went into the temple of light and received energetic organ replacements.

I flashback to when I was six or seven, I'm barefoot in the front yard wearing light blue matching seersucker shorts and top. Licking a dripping Popsicle, I realize the only reason I'm alive is because of the angels. I never thought much about it; it just seemed normal and natural.

My half-eaten apple abandoned, thrown in the garbage, and the ensuing inner battle consumed all of my resources.

My left brain is screaming, filled with fear, not knowing what to do. Who are these beings giving me energetic organ transplants? I demand to know. How do I know if they are for my highest good? How do I know if they're evil? My mind races, filled with worry and distress. Distraught, I don't know what to do. There is no concrete, logical proof that whoever has been doing this has my best interests in mind. My left brain demands that the organ transplants stop immediately. That day, the transplants stopped.

My health declined rapidly. A few months later, I started throwing up. In the beginning, I vomited for twelve to eighteen hours straight. Radioactive projectile puke belches from my guts. I kept getting sicker and sicker, for decades as the pain mounted.

Vomiting is a side effect of nuclear radiation. Plutonium radiation travels to the bones, making them weak and vulnerable. Bone cancer killed my Dad. I don't remember how many bones I've broken—collarbone, wrist, fingers, ribs, ankles, legs, toes.

My crutches are useless; it's too difficult to stand. My knees ache from rug burns, crawling on the carpet, dragging my broken foot behind me. The floor is dotted with bowls of half-eaten food, covered in irradiated puke. For five days and nights, radioactive vomit hurls, a heaving arch, filled with toxic debris spews—my bed, splattered with barf. Radiation seeps out of my broken ankle bone.

Nuclear waste drips down my blouse. I'm spread out on the nondescript beige carpet, close to the kitchen, face-up, praying to die —the refrigerator hums. Out the sliding glass doors, the sun shines, rare for a Seattle winter day. Beyond hope, I surrender. I imagine my rotting, dead body, dripping with nuclear waste, the house a fright. Who will clean up the mess?

It takes me years to put the two together, the puking my guts out, and the lack of energetic organ transplants. I don't know how to ask for and receive transplants again. I'm scared. I'm aware of other realms of nasty, creepy shit that I was oblivious to when I was a kid. As a child, I trusted the angels; they were my best friends. They were my safe haven at night, which counterbalanced my daily world of violence. When fear grips me, higher brain functions are usurped, leaving me incapable of connecting with the angelic realms. It's how our brains are currently wired.

Fear shut down my clear access to the dimension where the transplants take place. What I can do with my clients, I don't know how to access within myself. There is too much radiation in my body to sort out my inner seeing from the annihilation frequency of plutonium. Held in fear's grip, I'm caught up in day-to-day survival. It didn't occur to me to bring the multiple dimensions to my left brain to scrutinize, clear, name, and categorize.

COBRAS AND CAVES
1994

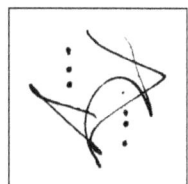

The fishhook of the beloved pierces my heart and reels me to India. I can fight and flap around like a half-dead fish, or I can surrender and follow this magnetized pull. I'm not hunting for a guru, much less in India. When I left India when I was eighteen, in 1964, I vowed never to return; to me, it was the most deplorable place on earth. It stuns my family to hear that I am returning to India. I, too, am shocked, but the sacred yearning inside is more potent than my mind's complaints.

On the train from New Delhi to Lucknow in Northern India, we pass small villages, oxen-plowed fields, and green terrain plots. The countryside is overlaid with a devout reverence; the contrast of physical poverty and religious richness is striking. Temples glisten in the sun, shacks made of cardboard and discarded bits of metal house entire families; spirituality and poverty mix together—the train's rhythmic referee, enhanced with *"Atlantis Angelis"* by Patrick Bernhardt playing on my new portable cassette player.

Small patches of crops dot the landscape, animals roam, and women in bright saris carry baskets on their heads. Brilliant red, orange, and azure saris drip with color. Colors ripple, flowing out beyond the fabric. Dr. Amber's quote, "Color is to the soul as air is to the body," swirls through my head. India is a land of the soul. Deep devotion and joy to the divine permeate the soil. Sacred pursuits are of the highest order, rather than the frantic financial stalking of the West.

India, the land of extremes, reflects the dichotomy of my inner landscape. Floating through this atmosphere saturated with the divine and beauty, I'm absorbing a sacred texture. The gut-wrenching poverty, mirroring my feeling like a failure, is horrifying. Guilt, shame, and lack of self-worth mingle, sabotaging my life. I know there has to be more to life than this inner turmoil. The silence of the ashram will help to quell this internal conflict.

In Lucknow, a porter grabs my suitcase, sticks it on his head, and runs through the crowds. I'm yelling, chasing after him as fast as I can, pushing my way through the masses. All the stuff in my suitcase is worth a small fortune in India and can disappear in a second. The porter stops at his friend's bicycle-driven rickshaw; I pay him and give the driver the address of Papaji's meeting hall. I'm off to see H.W.L. Poonja, lovingly called Papaji, one of Sri Ramana Maharishi's few living devotees.

My pale fingers hold a lavender-colored scarf over my face, blocking out the stench and bugs. My blue eyes peek over the veil, taking in the sights. The taxi weaves through cows, pigs in mud eating garbage, motorcycles, bicycles, and trucks decorated with fringe and gewgaws, all going in different directions, paying no attention to traffic flow. Wrapping a lock of sandy blonde hair behind my right ear, I contemplate why on earth I'm back in India. I've looked for answers from friends, family, and religion. Nothing fit. I want to know what is beyond fear and failure. Searching within, following the path of my heart, rather than my logical mind, it feels radical, exciting, and scary.

A green metal gate opens to the terra cotta-colored courtyard and deserted meditation hall. Fear sets in, I've traveled halfway around the world, and no one is here. Finally, on the roof, I find a few people eating at an organic restaurant for Papaji's devotees. They direct me to my guesthouse a few blocks away.

I have a roommate at the guesthouse. I hide when the radiation kicks in, but I've no place to go. Radioactive puke spurts from my guts for twelve hours straight, expelling everything, dry heaves take over. My roommate has never seen such a sight and wants me to go to the hospital. I explain this is normal; it's been happening every month for years.

It's never quiet in India. Each night, devotees from different religions drive the streets with huge speakers blaring scriptures or chanting, setting off the street dogs, which bark most of the night.

Hundreds of Americans and Europeans fill the meditation hall; *Satsang* is in English. *Satsang* is the Sanskrit term for gathering together for the truth. The regulars bring small cushions, and the rest of us sit on the bare cement floor. Sitting at the feet of Papaji, he gives me the name Ram Pyari, 'Beloved of God' or 'Love of God."

Papaji's laugh is contagious, and he says, 'Enjoy' every time I see him. I've come to India for profound sacred teachings, but it's rugby season. Papaji brings a TV to the Satsang hall and watches the games, with no spiritual or metaphysical insights revealed. A bit frustrated by rugby season, every day I read more of Ramana's books, the fire within deepens.

Splitting heartbreak intensifies, and I yearn to go to Sri Ramana Ashram at the foot of sacred Mount Arunachala. I swoon with adoration every time I read Ramana's one hundred and eight love poems to Mt. Arunachala. Something I'd never witnessed or experienced in the States, devotion, and depth of loving surrender that leaves my heart wide open and knows no bounds. With Papaji's blessings, I take off for Southern India.

The taxi passes three women laughing, baskets of golden wheat on their heads, scarlet, fuchsia, and turquoise saris swirl in the warm breeze. Radiant faces, with a dot of sacred ash on their foreheads, beam with joy and beauty. It's harrowing watching the driver pass a truck, squeeze in between two trucks, as a bus barrels full speed headed straight for the taxi. Fried nerves. Lying down in the back seat, curled up, rocked by the lurching taxi, beeping horns are my lullaby on the four-hour taxi ride from Chennai Airport to Tiruvannamalai.

I'm wearing a traditional Indian outfit of a *salwar* (pants) *kameez* (knee-length shirt), long scarf, and sandals. The pants, tight at the ankle, keep the bugs from crawling up my legs, baggy around my belly expanding enough for a pregnant woman, held up with a string. I use the long scarf to keep bugs off my face and protect my nose from noxious smells.

We stop at a little stand to pee and buy a drink. I smell the outhouse shack at least fifteen feet away. A hot box made of corrugated metal sheets with a tilted door hanging on one hinge hides a hole in the floor; a spigot hangs low on the wall.

I turn my fanny pack around to my stomach, pull up my *kameez*, pull down my *shalwar* and underpants, my scarf drops off my shoulder, and I hold all the fabric, so nothing hits the floor. My passport is strapped around my waist in a pouch with a few one-hundred-dollar bills. I'm gagging from the stench. To gain my balance, I want to use the wall for support, but filthy handprints cover the surface. There are places to put my feet; I squat down, my pee hits the edge of the hole, and squirts on my toes.

The custom is to wipe your butt with your left hand and wash it off. I'm prepared with toilet paper. I can't imagine how many bacteria thrive on the faucet handle. Wobbling from the stench, I bolt out of the bathroom, fanny pack awry; my dress caught up in my passport holder. I stagger to the soda pop stand to buy the driver a drink.

Coke, Fanta in various colors, and bottled water swim in a white rectangular metal Coca-Cola ice bucket with a rusty rim. The bottled water is questionable at places like this. The owners keep the empty bottles, fill them with tap water, and put a dab of superglue on the top to make you think it's factory sealed.

Back in the taxi, we pass villages with some kitchens covered in black soot. Bars on the windows, a locked gate for the door, and kitchens are separate rooms from the house. If the husband decides that his wife has done something he doesn't like, he will lock her in the kitchen and set her on fire. Unable to escape, she burns to death. And then, he finds a new wife and collects another dowry. Women are of such low status that men expect women to bring money or property to marriage—this has happened worldwide throughout history.

More honking horns and swerving around buses and trucks and Mt. Arunachala appears in the distance. The legend is that Shiva concealed his luminescent form and manifested himself as Arunachala so others could obtain illumination. In the Hindu tradition, Shiva is the auspicious one, regarded as limitless, transcendent, unchanging, and formless.

I arrived in Tiruvannamalai, known as Tiru, on the second day of the holy time of Deepam. I've missed the first day of Deepam, where millions of pilgrims swarm to town to circumambulate sacred Arunachala in sincere devotion and joy. A flame burns on Arunachala's summit, one of India's oldest living festivals, dating back to 2500 B.C. Ghee or clarified butter is carried to the top of the mountain and lit; the fire burns as long as the ghee lasts, usually about ten days and nights.

The Deepam festival signifies the unity of man and God; the two merge into one. The promise is that during Deepam, Mt. Arunachala opens up one's heart and reveals the self seated in the center of the heart's cave.

Outside the ashram's whitewashed walls, chaos ensues with people milling about, enveloped in the putrid smell of diesel exhaust, stinky animals, rotting garbage, and excrement. The ashram gates open to a large courtyard. Inside, the rarified air fills with the frequency of Sri Ramana Maharishi's grace. He died in 1950, but his presence is palpable.

To the left, a man sits in a shack protecting shoes. Inside the ashram gates, being barefoot is recommended and required in the halls. I slip my sandals into my bag rather than leaving them with the guard. Small, sharp rocks jab my tender feet. A woman with twigs tied to a short stick stoops over to sweep the dirt. Screeching peacocks strut brilliant turquoise, cobalt, and chartreuse feathers. All senses are assaulted to the point of full potency.

It's lunch, and *Sadhus*, holy men of India, with wild eyes, colored ash on their foreheads, unkempt hair, dressed in saffron robes, line up for food inside the front gate. Spiritual enlightenment, regarded as the highest goal in life, there is a long tradition of 'divine madness' in India. Since time immemorial, Indian society supports the holy men, for they are not supposed to work. There is no such system for women.

Past the *Sadhus* are the office and bookstore, and up the stairs to the left are Ramana's and his mother's sacred burial halls and the meditation room. The sweet smell of sandalwood wafts, light dapples through the trees.

'Who am I' is the core of Ramana's teaching. Getting rid of the 'I am the body' idea and merging the mind into the heart to realize the self as a non-dual being is the practice's focus. Ramana's presence envelops all.

The director of the ashram arrives and shows me to my room. Monkeys shriek outside; metal bars guard the one window. The bed is a two-inch-thick hard mattress covered with a bottom sheet and a bedspread. I wonder when the bedspread was washed. The bathroom has a drain in the center and two places for feet, with a sizable stinking hole in the middle. A small spigot is on the wall low, near the gaping cavity. Malaria-carrying mosquitoes fill the room.

Outside the dining room is a long cement trough with a row of faucets to wash your hands before and after eating. Walking into the dining room, I am overcome with divine grace, an expansive empty room with barred open windows that keep the screaming monkeys out.

Legs crossed, sitting on the austere cement floor, a brilliant green banana leaf and a small silver metal glass with a curved out rim are in front of me. No silverware; everyone eats with his or her right hand. Lined up in rows, each devotee sits in silence in front of a bare banana leaf. The first row is for foreigners, those without the inner fortitude to withstand the intense, hot food Indians love. Each devotee, absorbed in silence, sits in his or her world, not paying attention to anyone else. I sneak a peek and notice I'm one of the few foreigners and the only Western woman; this was before Tiruvannamalai became a spiritual tourism destination.

A young man walks down the row holding the thin handle of a large galvanized metal bucket and places a ladle of fluffy rice on the leaf. A man with a curry bucket follows, and then another with *raita*, a cucumber, and yogurt condiment to cool the palate. The curry is placed in the center of the rice pile, creating a dip to hold the flowing sauce. The liquid trickles until stopped by a ridge on the banana leaf. The ashram's director arrives with a long-spouted small pitcher filled with ghee or clarified butter. Each person receives a few swirls of ghee.

The aroma wafts as I lean over the food. The fragrance of rich, earthy curry spices follows sweet cinnamon. My fingers cascade into slippery ghee, flowing coconut-based curry swirls around veggies, long grains of well-formed, soft rice drink in the sauce. My fingers come together and scoop up the rice, succulent, spicy sauce, and veggies prepared with love. I consume the food with gusto, and luscious food drips down my throat. Spicy, fiery curry follows a refreshing cucumber and yogurt mixture filled with subtle spices. Curry slithers between my fingers, juice running. My fingers dive into the food mound, surfacing with more tasty morsels to devour.

I emerge from the meditation hall; the flame on top of Arunachala burns, illuminating a streak in the fading sky. The small stones on the well-swept-packed dirt are sharp. I'm picking my way through the larger spiky pebbles, treading with care, around the corner towards my room. I pass a group of wild monkeys that snatch people's bags in search of food.

In front of me, taking up the entire width of the path is a gigantic coiled cobra, head raised for action. Beady eyes, flicking tongue darting back and forth, in and out, head slowly moving from side to side, checking me out, ready to strike. My heart stops; I'm terrified of snakes. I take a deep breath. To the cobra's right is a high wall; on the left, a pool of wretched stagnant water covered with two inches of bacteria-filled green slime. Stepping backward, not turning to check on the monkeys, my eyes lock on the cobra's eyes. The darting tongue quickens. The snake is ready to elongate, reach out, and strike. I recede around the corner, back to the meditation hall.

Since arriving in India, I've been sitting meditating for weeks on bare shimmering floors, and my ankle bones are raw. A sharp pain runs up my sitz bones. The altar covered with bright orange marigold garlands, sandalwood incense fills the air; overcome with grace, I prostrate my full body on the cold, glistening floor. I didn't know I had it in me to experience this level of devotion. It just was, no struggle or effort, I followed the strings yanking on my heart.

The cobra is gone when I leave the meditation hall; I have a safe passage to my room.

The next morning, my heart's longing pulls me to Skanda Ashram, a cave in Mt. Arunachala where Ramana lived and meditated. I'm alone on the rocky, winding path, mesmerized and scared; I stand still. Undulating purple, silver, and shimmering fuchsia colors, a small snake slithers ahead on the trail. A group of women stop planting tiny trees on the hillside and watch me with a wary eye. The women yell. One woman runs full speed, shovel raised between both hands, and chops the snake into tiny sections. Shaken, I sidestep the squirming pieces of deadly viper and walk in silence to the cave.

I reflect on two deadly snakes on my path, a cobra and a viper. Are they tests of my devotion, a warning, or reminders of the serpent power related to Shakti?

A guard waits outside the gate to the cave, looking for seekers and money. Plants line the swept dirt courtyard; monkeys scurry searching for food. The mist evaporates, revealing Tiruvannamalai's spectacular panoramic view, the grand temple for Lord Shiva, Arul-

Cosmic Inner Seeing

migu Aruachaleswarar, below. To my right is a small whitewashed room where Ramana's mother lived and took care of his needs, cooking, cleaning, and washing. Freshly painted, green metal bars line the windows of Ramana's quarters, at the back, the innermost cave where he sat in meditation. Ramana lived here until his mother's death. Women aren't permitted burial on sacred ground, so Ramana moved off the hill and created Sri Ramana Ashram at his mother's gravesite.

Hundreds of thousands of spiritual seekers are on the street, walking the eight-mile journey between villages, from one marigold-adorned altar to the next, slowly moving, chanting, seeking connection to Shiva. Vibrant waves of devotion surround the hill with sublime, refined energy. I'm alone in Ramana's meditation cave, the size of a big bathtub, carved into the heart of Arunachala. My bare palms and soles drink in Arunachala's fire; I invite Shiva to seep into my body. In a flash, Shiva's luminosity ascends my body and flares out the top of my head.

For years, since my spontaneous Kundalini awakening, Shakti's force pounds, clearing my Ida and Pingala, the two channels that undulate through my body, like the double helix of DNA. The surge of Shiva's fire ignites my Shakti to flow with full force.

I leave the cave, walk down the hill, and out on the street, squalid beggars, who usually give me the Willies and make my skin crawl, become beautiful. I'm floating above the filth and stench; my feet barely touch the ground. The plight of the beggars becomes irrelevant as I see beauty everywhere.

The dirtiest, smelly, crawling with bugs places shift into a dazzling delight. Somehow, even the putrid smell is non-offensive. The disgusting turns into awe, grace, and beauty. Radiance drenches everything. I exist in an illuminated state of ecstatic sublime, bliss, and gratitude. Everything is alive and pulsating, bathed in a luminous luster. From this vantage point, others' pain and suffering pale compared to my upper body ecstatic bliss. There are stories of Ramana being in such euphoria that rats ate his flesh, and he had to be fed to stay alive.

At the main ashram, next to Ramana's former living quarters, is a massive marble sculpture. On a pedestal, at heart level, is a round, six-foot wide-open 1000-petal lotus. A magnificent phallus rises from the center. The lotus represents the crown chakra at the top of the head and signifies spiritual illumination. The tip of the lingam, adorned with marigolds and jasmine flowers, lines up with Arunachala's peak. The phallus erupts out of the lotus, connecting to God. My finger glides along the edge of the cool, smooth, long petals, sliding down one petal towards the large, erect, hard phallus—the sweet smell of sandalwood trails out of the meditation hall.

Shakti, the feminine energy at the base of the spine related to transformation, evolution, and awakening, is directed out of the top of the head. For eons, the goal has been to take this precious feminine energy, sit straight, spine erect, crossed legs, bring the frequency up the spine, out the top of the head, connecting to male authority.

I am out of my mind and body in a state of bliss, nirvana, Satori, one-ness, one with the Beloved. I'm in a state beyond suffering, desire, and sense of self, devoted to someone or something outside of myself.

The state the mystics write about is divine rapture, an illuminated consciousness many long to achieve. A dissolving occurs; there is only the Beloved residing in my heart, no guru, no separate being. Ramana and I are one. Usually, the glimpses last for fleeting moments or even a few hours. After experiencing this depth of love and joy, there is a natural tendency to want more.

I become aware of a large disk about twelve inches above my head, denying me access to the angelic realms and higher dimensions. An unseen pathway, on my right side, at a 66-degree angle, siphons off my Shakti. A spiritual bypass, an energetic cut, siphoning off my energy into the old paradigm. In exchange, I feel euphoric.

Cosmic Inner Seeing

I exist in this exalted state that so many devote their lives to achieve. The spiritual becomes more important than the physical, creating an imbalance, a top-heavy reality where the lower part of my body is left behind. I'm sucked into the grip of leaving behind my precious essence for a heady, unsustainable state of nirvana. This state depends on renouncing the feminine and siphoning off the feminine life force. Seduced into the spiritual quest searching outside myself, I further deny my value and worth. I attain the pinnacle of spiritual seeking, only to discover it's not what I want.

The ecstasy and bliss come at a very high price, the price of disconnection and violence. The problem is that this spiritual awakening is partially out of my body. The body is denied in this tradition, making it less important than the spiritual. This energy then feeds the forces that keep violence, self-disrespect, and fear in motion. This practice, passed down since the beginning of patriarchy, continues today.

By my eighth day in this revered state, the novelty thoroughly explored, I wanted my connection with the angels back. It becomes clear this awakening is not what I am searching for.

I want whole body awakening.

My path is not one of disconnection but of diving deep into the feminine mysteries residing in the lower part of my body.

The internal fire continues to blaze. I feel like a loaf of half-baked bread yanked from the oven, but I must return to the States; personal commitments wait. I've been gone for almost two months, and I've run out of money.

After an hour of playing chicken with buses and trucks, the taxi slows down. I'm wondering why we are stopping; I have a plane to catch. A lone tree shades a small altar. The driver pops out and sits down to meditate.

The carving on the altar is a woman with a giant red tongue sticking out, wearing a necklace of skulls, and four arms, one holding a sword, another holding a head dripping blood. She's dancing on a man's body. I recognize the image; it's the Hindu goddess Kali. Kali is the fierce aspect of the divine feminine, associated with Shakti, the power of creation, destruction, and evolution. Kali is the destroyer of evil, the most powerful form of Shakti. Kali stands on her reclining husband, Shiva, the unchanging, formless, and limitless God.

Looking around the taxi, I notice the rearview mirror, surrounded by fuzzy red fake fur, draped with prayer beads. Small pictures of Kali decorate the dashboard, and bright orange fringe hangs along the top of the front window. After ten minutes, the driver returns to the car and drives towards the airport, without saying a word.

As the taxi lunges forward, I reflect on my time in India. Shiva's illuminating fire, Kali's devouring with love, and Shakti's feminine creative power contribute to my great unraveling. One of the most exquisite gifts I receive is to learn about gratitude. An intensity of gratitude that burrows into my core, it's nothing like the skin-deep thanks acknowledged in the States. This gratefulness pierces beyond anger, wretchedness, fear, and terror, down to the depths of love and nourishes my being in ways never known before.

I am a different person from the one arriving in India a few months ago. Radiant, I glide into Chennai airport wearing a light lavender hand-embroidered *salwar kameez*, my scarf flowing in the breeze, a *bindi* on my forehead, and a piercing gaze. The ticket agent, without my asking, upgraded my seat compliments of the airline.

In the San Francisco airport, the customs official mocks me and demands I chant before he stamps my passport and grants me re-entry into the States. Welcome home. For me, the culture shock of the States is always more painful and difficult than the culture shock of being in a foreign country.

NO MIND
1995

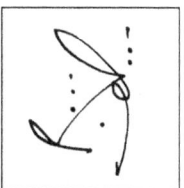

India's sun and heat turn into soggy, dull grey; the spiritual frequency of India melts off in the drizzle. My slow, reflective pace of sitting in silence is jarred by the caffeine-driven buzz and computer hum of Seattle.

My awakening in India was like turning on the light in a long-neglected basement; my expanded consciousness exposed layers of the unconscious. My illuminated state dissolves, uncovering concealed, suppressed fright.

Immobilized by terror, I want to escape and sit in silence. Beyond worry and thoughts of failure, past childhood trauma, the inner horror movie flickers behind all known fears, every shred of me devoured in the panic of annihilation. Had I stayed longer in India, would the fire of Arunachala have burned away the dross?

Not knowing what to do, my decades of spiritual conditioning kicked in. At my altar, facing photos of Arunachala and Ramana, I chant Ramana's name. In the microscopic space between the words Ramana and Ramana, the Earth splits in two, revealing a chasm filled with a vicious onslaught of annihilating terror. I'm engulfed in black horror, not a speck of light is seen. I'm in a death grip on the river of darkness. I call on Ramana, pursue ancient traditions, watch a candle, and follow breathing exercises. Nothing helps.

I want to break out, go out the top of my head, escape to heaven, and get the hell out of my body. Past the dread of grotesque demons, ghoulish monsters, faces dissolving in flames, flesh dripping off bones, radioactive dismemberment of the souls of Hiroshima. Fire rages within, the heat and turmoil in my spine amaze bodyworkers, and doctors put me on anti-inflammatories. Nothing helps.

Flames devour me, past regions of torture chambers, through eons of blazing terror into the black void. My unconscious is the fright garbage dump, holder of bomb residue. The terror feels much bigger than me. Is this the horror from the souls of Hiroshima? Beyond the land of soul-sucking entities, inner screams echo through the thick black nothingness of annihilation.

After four months of immobilizing panic, I need to work; my money has dried up. I found a job selling fabric and interior design textiles. On my eighth day at work, I lifted a bolt of cloth and hurt my back. Three days later, I can't move or sleep. My right arm is numb, followed by sharp pains down my right leg. I wake in the night, screaming. I've lost my ability to talk, and my memory has vanished.

Dr. Robertson's office is around the corner. Framed posters of snow-capped mountains line the waiting room walls; it takes me a long time to fill out the forms. I riffle through bits of paper in my wallet to find my Social Security number. I look at my checkbook to see my address and phone number. When complete, I attempt to read a magazine. Words are too difficult; I find one full of pictures and wait. Finally, I'm escorted to an examination room.

"Hello, I'm Dr. Robertson. What can I do for you today?" he says while flipping through the pages of my intake form.

"I..." I can't remember what I'm saying.

"Well, it says here that you have a pain in your arm and neck. Can you tell me about the pain?" Dr. Robertson says.

I point to my neck. "Neck" comes out of my mouth. I say a word and then rumble around in a vast, cloudy space hunting for the next word. By the time I find the second word, the first word is gone. This second word has nothing to attach to. I am lost, forgot what I was saying. Stringing four words together is exhausting, tedious, and almost impossible.

Dr. Robertson studies my chart again. Later, he told me that he thought I was slow, maybe mentally challenged, until he looked at my intake form. In the education section, I checked the boxes that I graduated from college and have a Ph.D. When the doctor realized I had a Ph.D., he knew something was very wrong.

"Can you raise your right arm above your head for me?" the doctor asks.

I raise my arm slightly; flowing tears leave wet spots on my pink blouse. The doctor hands me a small box of Kleenex.

"Well, I think we have some serious trouble here. I'm going to take some tests and refer you to a specialist. I see you have insurance."

I nod, yes.

"Good, you don't have to worry about a thing. I'll submit all the insurance forms, and the receptionist will set up an appointment for you with a neurologist."

All the specialists, neurologists, MRIs, and tests reveal nothing.

The tormentors take over—every moment, a ghoulish figure, screams of horror, burning flesh dripping off rotting bones, the deepest, vast darkness. I couldn't take it anymore. My brain stopped. The gremlins, horror, and goblins had no way to get me. That part of my brain shut down, blocked off, bolted shut.

I'm like a small child. I comprehend enough to get dressed, eat, and go to sleep when it is dark. I have no idea if I even comb my hair. Getting the laundry in both the washer and the dryer on the same day is a miracle.

The light inches across the wall, shifting shadows, varying shades. I've been sitting in the same chair perhaps all day; I must have gone to the bathroom, I don't remember.

Inflammation rages, burning through the protective coating around my nerves. The part of my brain that perceived the terror and nasty goblins shut down. It was too much for my physical form to withstand. My neocortex and left brain are crippled. My amygdala, the part of the brain that produces automatic responses associated with fear, is disabled. The terror and trauma went so deep that my brain disconnected itself as a survival mechanism. The pain remains, but the terror vanishes. I can't worry or be afraid, the pathway to the fear center in my reptilian brain shuts down—other bundles of neurons and areas of my brain marginally function.

Like a camera stuck to the top of my head, a witnessing emerges, viewing events with no action or judgment, the nonjudgmental observer. All brain processes related to reasoning and analysis no longer function. The witness bypasses my brain, heart, and guts, and observes with no judgment, no feeling, and no connection. Neutral to everything that is arising, the spiritual tradition of non-attachment is what many people strive to achieve. The part of the brain that many spiritual practices encourage activating. There is no ego to keep me safe and functioning—no mental chatter.

Inner peace, almost happiness, from being so simple-minded emerges. I'm like a small developmentally disabled child, only with massive pain. Energetic nuclear bombs explode in my occiput like Mexican fireworks. Toxic radioactive cells squirt battery acid throughout my brain. Inflammation in my neck ignites a fire in the battery acid coursing through my head. The torture continues.

I have the mental capacity of a two-year-old. I don't know how to balance a checkbook or dial a telephone. I do know how to tie my shoes.

Pale pink and orange, subtle colors, and textures of light move across the wall, broadcasting the day. Later, the wall turns gray with a tint of radiant blue peeking through.

My sense of direction vanishes. In the past, I wandered alone in the remote wilderness for days with no map or compass and always found my way. Now, walking down a street I have known for years, I am lost.

More test results still reveal no problem. Physical therapy is useless. The doctors led me down a dark path of prescription drugs and no answers. They prescribe more pills, narcotics, painkillers, and antidepressants. My mind doesn't work; in desperation, I take the

Cosmic Inner Seeing

drugs. Drugs cure nothing; they are manufactured to cover up symptoms, make me dependent, and make me a lifelong customer.

I start collapsing. There is a moment of warning before I crumple, and suddenly, all the life force runs out of my body. I can't move, my legs buckle, and I crumble to the floor. I don't lose consciousness like when I pass out; I'm conscious the whole time, I just can't move. I can't even crawl to the couch. Sometimes I'm sprawled out on the kitchen floor for three or four hours.

Speaking is next to impossible. I can't put a complete sentence together. I don't know how to ask for help. All I can do is stare at the light creeping across the wall.

Days pass into months, gray purple light moves across the wall, shifting patterns and shadows, changing color and intensity. Blue-gray light in the morning gains intensity and brightness at noon, the glimmer and gold of streaming late afternoon sunlight creating sparkles in the air. Later, the wall turns gray with a tint of radiant blue peeking through.

Around the corner is a small strip mall with professional offices. The sign says Network Chiropractic. I don't know what that is, but the energy of the place is intriguing. Dr. Marcus is young; his bright eyes display confidence. The small entry opens to a large room with five massage tables. Facedown on the tables, people are lined up like fish on a platter, ready to be served up. Dr. Marcus does a few light touches at the neck, wrist, and foot, and moves on to the next patient. I realize he sees and works on many dimensions and layers.

After my first visit, the pain in my right foot diminished. I know this treatment will help. The light touch allows my body to find a different route and establish new neural connections, not based on fear and terror but based on my essence.

The collective unconscious fear and terror stored in my body were released for nine months. It takes about a year for my speech to return. By my fiftieth birthday, I can carry on a conversation, nothing very articulate or scientific, but I can string a bunch of sentences together.

I descended into the unconscious realms, unable to speak for almost a year, watching the light inch across the wall, almost comatose. The monsters were sure to have their way with me, scare the living daylights out of me. Make me crazy. I survived; Shakti's evolutionary energy surges through my body, demanding the return of my left brain functioning.

By some miracle, I financially slid through on my IRS refund, maxing out my credit card, and a lot of divine intervention.

Preparing to write this book, I check all the dates stamped in my passports to make sure I remember everything correctly. I found visa stamps for Guatemala in 1974. A completely forgotten trip, memories flood in, flying in a used war-torn cargo plane, rope woven seats with no backs, sticking my finger through the bullet holes in the side of the plane, cruising low over the jungle to a landing strip near the ancient ruins of Tikal.

What chunks of my life are erased, whisked away, never to return? I have no idea.

SEATTLE NEEDLES
1998

As my memory returns, a more profound pain that has always been present intensifies. My cells feel large, swollen, emitting a radioactive, toxic, needle-like energy. The pain is hot and dull. It feels like a contaminated Brillo pad is jammed between each cell. My pelvic bones are on fire; a red-hot branding iron wedged deep inside my skin. A radioactive claw squeezes my thyroid, shutting down its functioning.

The gremlins are always there, poking, screaming, I'm fucked up, shouting that I'm worthless. And then pain vies for my attention, a continuous barrage of junk and crap. I want to be done with all of this. I want to jump out of my skin so the jagged shaking of the radiation will stop. I cannot differentiate the toxins from the real me; I only know how to keep quiet and hide. Radiation has a quality of self-loathing and craziness that is hard to deny. During moments when the radiation is coming out, I can comprehend how someone could commit mass murder.

I've spent most of my life going to doctors trying to figure out what was wrong with me. Some doctors won't admit they know nothing about radiation toxicity; others look at me dazed. Financial stress is the usual diagnosis. Have you ever heard of anyone puking his or her guts out for twelve to eighteen hours straight, every month,

DR. CYNTHIA MILLER

for years, because of financial stress? One doctor broke out in tears when I told her my story, but had nothing to offer. Along with traditional Western medicine, I have tried every conceivable therapy, treatment, herbal supplement, pill, tonic, practice, food combination, alternative therapy, ritual, meditation practice, and ceremony.

Tears flow down my cheeks, trying to wash away the deep pain. My breath is short, cut off, and shallow. Hopelessness sets in. I want to crawl into a hole and hide, hide all the ugliness, hide all the pain, and hide the radiation.

I know I'm full of radiation; when I turn things on, they explode. One day, as I reach out to turn on my Apple computer, I watch a green neon spark jump out of my finger headed for the on button. Wires crackle, smoke erupts, and a popping sound. The repairman keeps insisting that my computer was struck by lightning.

My indigo iMac computer, shaped like a fat bug, with a semi-transparent plastic case, had tubes similar to a TV. All the tubes are fried. It's useless to explain that all I did was turn it on. I've blown up three computers, countless toasters, vacuum cleaners, and washing machines. I fix everything with my handy soldering iron, except the computers.

Dr. Smyth's office is tucked away from foot traffic, two blocks from Lake Washington. I'm nervous and wary of seeing another doctor, but I'm tired of the pain, feeling like crap, and puking my guts out. Walking into the doctor's small green office, I feel at ease.

I learned that in 1986, Dr. Smyth was on active duty and sent to Chernobyl after the nuclear reactor incident to clean up the mess. He became ill. After he tried different treatments, he discovered that chelation therapy worked for him. Chelation therapy is a medical procedure where a substance is injected into the body to grab or bind with heavy metal toxins.

My body relaxes. Oh, thank goodness, the doctor knows what he is talking about; he has personal experience.

My lab results reveal severe heavy metal toxicity, extremely high plutonium and uranium levels, and other problems.

Every treatment is the same. My naked body is stretched out on the clean strip of paper that runs down the center of the black examination table. Instead of a regular syringe, the needle is hooked up to an eight-foot rubber tube attached to a large mason jar with a mixture of DMPS and procaine.

Procaine is similar to Novocaine, which dentists use, and makes me numb. DMPS stands for "2,3-dimercapto-1-propanesulfonic acid sodium", also known as Dimovol, is a synthetic amino acid chelating agent of toxic heavy metals, which forms a water-soluble complex with toxic heavy metals.

Dr. Smyth begins with what he calls "the crown of thorns." Shots start in my forehead and circle my skull, like the paintings of Jesus with thorns dripping blood down his face. Then the sharp tip of the needle jabs into the delicate skin around my eye, stuck in at an angle to miss my eyeball. The shots continue down my face, each shot more painful than the last.

The one tiny window is always closed, so people on the street can't hear my screams. Kicking and hollering, I clutch the edge of the padded black table. Then more shots down my neck. He presses spots on my shoulders and shoots up the ones that hurt the most.

I notice the massive callus on his thumb. The doctor has to push an entire jar full of concoction through a skinny needle into my body. Needle pricks down my arms into my hands and between my fingers. Shots around my lungs and breasts, then I turn over for shots down my spine. I'm flopping back and forth, front to back like a screaming radioactive fish.

Then the doctor turns around and changes the needle. He tries to hide the long needle that goes all the way into my ovaries. I'm howling, legs flying, gasping for air.

He changes back to the shorter needle and heads for my genitals —the radiation lodges in my bones and sex cells. There are a few spots near my labia that kill me with endless pain, a hard lump of toxins, and plutonium. Dr. Smyth is young and virile; I'm so embarrassed I can't say the words; I point to where I want the excruciating injections. The dull needle stabs continue, down my legs, Achilles tendon, between my toes, and the soles of my feet.

It takes an hour to receive about one hundred shots; this is repeated weekly for eighteen months. By the time I'm dressed and out the door, I'm feeling pretty good; the procaine has kicked in. Finally, back home, no pain, just delicious freedom and joy.

The roller coaster ride begins. I enjoy hours of blessed relief; then, as the radiation comes out of my body, all hell breaks loose. Pain and ecstasy, feeling like shit, then a whiff of bliss—back and forth, I bounce as the radiation comes out in layers.

The radioactive and heavy metal toxins start to physically exit my body through my urine and energetically out of my genitals. Invisible hot molten lava flows out of my vagina, searing my inner thighs, dripping down, forming a puddle of radioactive debris at my feet. The pain is excruciating. The elastic on my underpants around my legs feels like it will melt.

I see a black tar-like substance covering the neon blue-green ball in my brain stem. The mass shrinks as I undergo the therapy. The energy that destroyed Hiroshima is locked in the tissues of my body. Rusted barbed wire rips through my brain. Rage spews from my guts. I feel like nasty scum. The radiation exudes out of my cells and drips down my gums and teeth, leaving a bitter metallic taste. "Please, God, kill me," is my nightly prayer.

What to do with all this rage? My heart is pounding red. How to pour out all the red without destroying myself, everything, and everyone around me? Remembering Kali from the taxi ride in India, I call on Kali, the Hindu goddess of destruction, the destroyer of evil forces. She wears a necklace of skulls, and her huge red tongue hangs. I invite the rage in and surrender to the volcanic eruption that is blasting through my body. The more I surrender, the greater the peace. The surrender flows into pulsating, joyous movement.

I flip between rage and peace. The anger is an old pattern passed down through the ages. The stone of violence, abuse, and fear was dropped into the pool of the human psyche long ago, and I feel its ripples. I tend to regress to the rage pattern, the rage habit that has dominated this planet for eons. This pattern is ingrained in every cell of my body, encoded in my DNA. But the peace is so expansive, a new, fresh space. I relax and spread out, awareness stretches beyond my body and extends into the consciousness of all that is. When the war stops inside, my body feels sensuous and flowing, like warm honey sweetly oozing or melting chocolate. The relief, the freedom of dropping deeper through the ripple, is pure bliss.

Over the next year and a half, I have about eighty visits to the doctor, which totals about 8,000 shots. Over half my salary is eaten up by these treatments; insurance pays nothing, and I'm led to believe that my radiation is gone.

The pain eased but didn't go away. I stopped blowing up toasters, vacuum cleaners, and washing machines when I turned them on. And, no more blown-up computers. The first computer I had was an Apple that looked like a bug, with tubes like an old TV. One day, I was feeling particularly crappy, as my index finger headed to push the on button, a huge spark of neon green energy flew out of my finger. Tubes erupted, smoke billowed; the repairman was sure the computer was hit by lightning.

Years later, I realize I'm not alone in my decades of futile attempts to uncover how to heal radiation. I discovered the Japanese weren't allowed to discuss what was happening in their bodies after being bombed. Russian soldiers, present at nuclear blasts, had to sign an affidavit saying they wouldn't talk about the effects of radiation on their bodies for twenty-five years. It's been a global agreement to abnegate the impact of nuclear radiation. The public has been denied access to critical information; for decades, global denial festers, creating more pain and suffering.

Throughout the chelation process, in the night, colors pulsate and throb in my body, demanding to be seen. I climb out of bed and muck around in color and water. Gooey paint moves and mingles as my hands slide and ooze across the paper. Energy wells up, pulsates, surges through my body, and shoots out my hands, as the paint squishes and slimes through my fingers. Sometimes I heave the paint, scratching lines with my fingernails. Now exhilarated, my juicy palms caress the paper, creating seemingly useless art. When the living room and dining room floors are covered in wet paintings, spent, I go back to bed. In the morning, most of the art ends up in the dumpster; a few pieces remain—relief at last. Forbidden radiation, held inside for decades, denied by mainstream medicine, kept quiet around the world, oozes onto the paper with delight. Unspoken words, prohibited energy seen, colors exposed, shapes revealed, and emotions expressed.

ASHES
2000

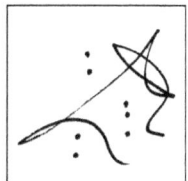

Mom's mantra of "Just don't think about it" became a reality. She develops dementia and Alzheimer's, just like her mother. For the last four years of her life, she has had no idea who I am.

She is kicked out of numerous nursing homes due to her behavior of running around naked, spreading her excrement on the walls, and swearing. The second to last time I saw her, she rubbed her shit-infested fingers on my face while telling me I am sweet, unaware of who I am. My mind is screaming, my body reeling, but I can't overcome the childhood neural patterns of being submissive to my mother. No amount of soap and water can scrub away that memory —what a fabulous metaphor for my relationship with my mother.

The last time I saw her, she was like a child. I comb her soft, silvery flaxen hair while she wraps her rubberized bed pad around her shoulders like a fancy cape. She curls up in my lap and falls asleep.

Weeks later, she stops swearing, and the attendants at the nursing home know something is wrong and take her to the hospital. Pneumonia has set in. I receive a call from the hospital; Mom is moving in and out of being present. The phone is placed next to Mom's ear. In a transcendent moment of clarity, I thank her for being my mother. I acknowledged all she had done for me. Three times, she slowly mutters, "I love you." For the first time in my life, I heard those precious three words. She died two days later.

At the crematorium, I want to watch my mother go up in flames. Crouched on the floor, peeping through the hole where the poker is jammed to light the gas, flames eat the cardboard box, licking their way towards her silver flaxen hair. It feels like I'm the one in the box burning, and I want to witness the event. I want to watch her body burn to the bone, but as the heat rises, I'm escorted out of the cremation chamber.

Human ashes are gritty, sharp, and jagged. At least that is how my parents' ashes felt. Two different times we created circular bits of toile tied with a ribbon, like the small packets of rice given out at weddings. The first time they held the ashes of my Dad, and years later, my Mom's. Their dust was scattered around their favorite place, the cabin; Dad's ashes by his treasured fishing streams, and Mom's remains around her cherished trees.

THE MANILA ENVELOPE
2000

The secrets in the manila envelope reveal mysteries of my life. When I receive the envelope, I can look at its contents for a few moments, and I become nauseous or dizzy, and stop reading. It takes years for me to have the courage to read everything it contains.

In 2000, after Mom's death, I inherited a 12" x 15" manila envelope. It contains a black leather-bound book meticulously compiled, organized, and typed by Dad's secretary, Dale. The black book includes charts, correspondence, travel records, and job descriptions. The packet holds top-secret information about my Dad's work, news clippings, badges, photos, passports, and reports.

I burned the derogatory poems defaming women written by various men at the South Pacific Proving Grounds.

A letter from President Harry Truman on White House stationery thanks my Dad for helping to bring about the total defeat of the enemy.

The envelope held maps of Hiroshima, with concentric circles radiating from the epicenter, measuring and tracking the destruction's magnitude. During the war, Hiroshima and Nagasaki were purposely not hit by warfare, so if the bomb was dropped, the damage could be measured with accuracy. The deadly weapon was designed to be released on Germany, but the peace treaty in Europe was signed on May 8, 1945. History reveals that the Japanese were getting ready to surrender. Once the peace treaties are signed, there is no excuse to bomb Japan. Dropping the bomb is an experiment that has to take place during a war, and time is running out.

Unusual official documents spill out of the packet; I call them bomb certificates, signed by officials representing the Army, Navy, Air Force, and the Atomic Energy Commission. I learned that Dad was the head construction engineer in charge of all nuclear warfare tests at the Nevada Test Site and the South Pacific Proving Grounds at Eniwetok. I knew he built bombs, but I had no idea of the extent of his destructive work. The further I dig into the contents, the more disgusted I become.

The bomb certificates look like a high school art project. At first, I thought each bomb certificate represented one bomb. Five years later, I discovered declassified information on the Internet about each of the six documents.

During Operation Ivy at Eniwetok in 1952, the Ivy-Mike hydrogen bomb produced a fireball more than three miles across. An island in the South Pacific was bombed into oblivion and vaporized, disappearing into a cloud that spread 150 square miles and dropped back into the ocean, creating radioactive fallout covering 800 square miles.

In 1954 Operation Castle series caused hundreds of radiation injuries and deaths while contaminating much of the Marshall Islands in the South Pacific.

This was the McCarthy era, and U.S. Sen. Joseph McCarthy of Wisconsin produced a series of investigations and hearings during the 1950s in an effort to expose the supposed communist infiltration of various areas of the U.S. government. From April to May 1954, Oppenheimer was interrogated and used as a scapegoat to promote the government's authority, fear, and control over the masses.

A few years before the investigations, Oppenheimer taught all the physics equations, wisdom, and secrets to my Dad, and three other men. My Dad was an unknown construction engineer, not one of the world-famous physicists, so he was the one chosen to be in charge of the construction of all the American nuclear warfare. The physicists were brilliant; my Dad was a creative genius.

After Oppenheimer was stripped of his security clearance and his career was in tatters, conversations at home were even more restricted. Keeping quiet clamped down quite a few notches at our house. We never spoke about politics, religion, philosophy, or any type of thinking. When I asked questions, Mom's response was always the same: "Just don't think about it" became engrained in our minds and thus our speech.

I was surprised one day in 1956 to find "I LIKE IKE" signs pounded in the front yard along the street. I don't think the name Eisenhower was mentioned in our house since we never discussed politics or the government. I didn't understand but was forbidden to ask, so I kept quiet. Now, looking back, I realize that President Eisenhower was in favor of building and testing nuclear warfare, so Dad was displaying his loyalty to the government.

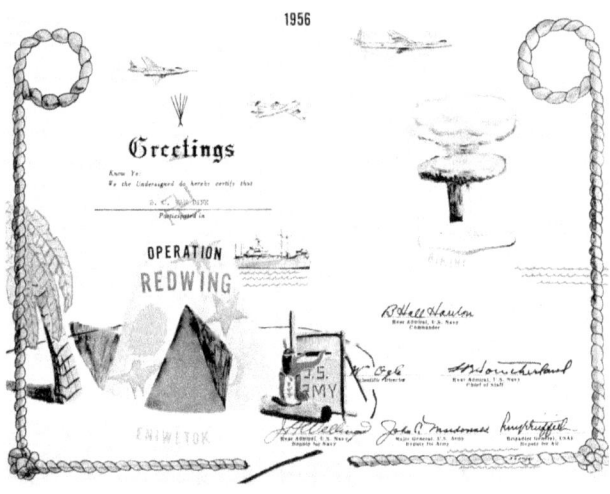

The Operation Redwing certificate, from 1956, has a teepee and a Native American weaving a blanket that says US Army. All the nuclear weapons in Operation Redwing were named after the Native American tribes. The arrogance of white male supremacy in choosing these names and being so insensitive makes my guts churn in disgust. The Native Americans, the original people of the land, who played such a key role in helping to keep America safe, are degraded by having bombs named after their tribes. The contempt I have for my father's cohorts grows.

One of the seventeen bombs dropped in the Operation Redwing

Cosmic Inner Seeing

series, the Seminole bomb, left a crater approximately 600 feet wide and 30 feet deep and sent frequencies that broke windows hundreds of miles away.

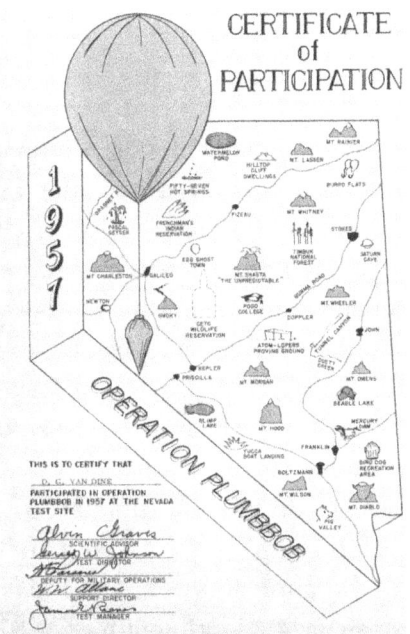

Operation Plumbbob in 1957 consisted of twenty-nine explosions at the Nevada Test Site; 1,200 pigs were subjected to biomedical experiments. Live pigs, placed in elevated cages, wearing suits made of different materials, test the best protection from the thermal blast. Other pigs were placed in pens at varying distances from the epicenter, behind large sheets of glass, to test the effects of flying debris on living targets.

At the Nevada test site, they built an entire city, houses filled with TVs, refrigerators, and stoves, manikins dressed in the latest clothes, and cars in the driveways. And then they blew it up. In another test in the South Pacific, they blew up an entire submarine filled with live sheep. Reading about these tests, I want to puke; this is the kind of crap American taxpayer dollars support.

Dad is fascinated with critical mass, creating a chain reaction, the yield of each bomb, how far the shockwaves spread, and how extensive the damage is. The more destructive and far-reaching, the better. His expertise was how to build the most significant bang of destruction for the smallest bucks. Plutioium-239 and uranium-235 are expensive to make.

Dad came home consumed with radiation, and as a small child, I picked up that specific frequency. Our bodies mimic the wiring of our parents. Repeated exposure to nuclear radiation became woven into my nervous system, enveloped in my cells, and lodged in my psyche. Each time Dad came home from watching another series of atomic explosions, his frequency altered radically. My body imprinted off his destructive and annihilation frequency, leading to a profound depth of self-loathing and massive, all-consuming sickness.

Some people assume that radiation washes off. Taking a shower and changing your clothes is not enough to clean up radioactive contamination. It's more like an internal sunburn; it doesn't dissolve in water. An atomic bomb is similar to a gargantuan blast of X-rays that leaves your innards vibrating at a destructive man-made frequency. The purpose of weapons-grade plutonium-239 is annihilation and death. That frequency creates an inner atmosphere of wanting to kill oneself, feeling worthless, and being unlovable.

Cosmic Inner Seeing

Operation Hardtack in 1958 had two series of tests, one at the Nevada Test Site, the other in Eniwetok, a total of seventy-two explosions, more nuclear detonations than the total of all prior nuclear explosions. A portion of the Nevada test site fallout traveled East. After Dad died, Mom moved to St. George, Utah, where the high levels of downwinder radiation made her feel at home.

The final document is from the Armed Forces Special Weapons Project in 1958, sun-bright yellow paper with an orange exploding bomb. On Google, I discovered that every man who received this certificate died of cancer, including my father.

Four women were required to hold up the image of my Dad. A man up on a pedestal higher than all of us, more competent than any of us could ever be, with greater power than any of us could ever dream of. Mom, Dad's secretary, Dale, my sister, and I were the silent, unacknowledged backdrop that created the perfect front for my father to be accepted and to do his work.

His job was far more critical and vital than any of us could ever be. He loved his work way more than family, home, or friends. I'm sure the rush of exploding bombs far outweighed any connection to his family or what a wife and kids could offer. Mom always said, thank goodness your Dad loves his work. In the 50's, the woman's role was to support her husband, no matter what. Her role was homemaking, which she loathed. She wanted to be a fashion designer. In her reality, she had no choice.

Home was the pit stop. Get laid, grab a few clean shirts, neatly paired socks, folded briefs, and dry-cleaned suits, and fly off to an unknown place on another secret mission. His brown leather zippered ditty bag, never unpacked, sat on the bathroom sink. At a moment's notice, his toothbrush and razor were ready to be packed into his silver Samsonite suitcase. No wonder my Mom was a raging alcoholic.

We were the cover he hid behind, the light to camouflage his destruction. My job was to keep quiet and allow him to siphon off my feminine energy to create his dastardly deeds. I learned that my role in life was to cover up for the man to spread my light over his darkness. That was the arrangement.

My childhood was filled with the deadliest frequencies of nuclear warfare. I was a sponge and incorporated the frequencies of annihilation and destruction into my nervous system, bones, muscles, and cellular structures.

Dad brought home radiation from at least 131 nuclear and atomic bomb tests. Depraved, convoluted, power-mongering, all under the guise of national security—this was back in the 50s. Imagine all the covert corruption, manipulation, and deception our US tax dollars fund today, all in a cover-up kept secret from the American public. Follow the money trail and discover what is happening behind the scenes.

Before the Cold War ended, an estimated 70,000 nuclear warheads were stockpiled by the world's nations. Atmospheric tests have released fallout equal to 40,000 Hiroshimas.

Cosmic Inner Seeing

When I was thirty, my parents visited me in Aspen, Colorado. On a beautiful summer day, we ate lunch on a balcony overlooking the ski resort; clouds dot the blue sky, and aspen trees murmur in the breeze. Unusual for my Dad, he volunteered to discuss his latest travel. He just returned from the Pentagon.

Pulled out of retirement, he was the only civilian at a high-level conference about how to store nuclear waste. The best containers last only one hundred years. Right now, containers of nuclear waste dumped in the ocean ooze radiation into the water—I flashback to when I was five and asked him who would clean up the mess. I keep quiet, wondering why it took them so long to address this problem.

Plutonium-239 has a half-life of about 24,110 years. That means that in 24,110 years, half of the initial plutonium will still generate toxicity. In another 24,1100 years, one-half of that will be inactive. That is a long time in our little lives. We survived the initial blasts, but there is no escaping the effects of plutonium toxicity that's eating away at our ecosystem, environment, food, and health. We will adapt or become extinct.

Recently, I learned that the crafty United States government created the Atomic Energy Commission, the AEC, as a private corporation so the government would not be responsible for the health of its citizens exposed to nuclear radiation.

My heritage is your legacy and heritage. All of humanity is affected every day by weapons-grade man-made radiation. War is a game played by power mongers without regard for the citizens and the global consequences. The low-frequency mentality that creates war also drives the current reality. We live in a world run by adult seven-year-old bullies who inject fear into our lives daily to gain more money, power, and control.

> As Einstein said, "We cannot solve our problems with the same thinking we used when we created them."

Either we are doomed to toxicity, which may be the case. Or, perhaps there is another side to the story. Humanity needs to mature beyond its current level of consciousness. As I dig deeper into how to evolve beyond killing each other, I discover it's outside the limits of our thinking, located on multi-dimensions, and encoded in our DNA and neurological programs.

EXPLODING ORGASMIC BOMBS
2000

It's my 54th birthday, and Byron Katie is in Seattle presenting 'The Work.' During the event, we are asked to say one line about something we think should be different. The microphone comes to me; "My Dad shouldn't drop bombs," is my statement. Katie asked me to stand in front of the 300-plus people in the room and say the statement plus the turnaround, "I shouldn't drop bombs."

When I get home, I feel shaky, weird, and nauseous, and lie down on the couch. I realize all the ways I drop bombs on people, not physical bombs, but words, emotions, or actions. Everything I judged in my father, I am doing. Quite shocking. With the release of the judgment, my cells discharge the pent-up frequencies of bombs.

The energy starts to build inside my body. At first, I'm uncomfortable and anxious. I want the intensity to get moving out of my body, so I wiggle around, and the energy moves up my spine. Bombs start exploding in my cells, and my genitals become hot. The power continues to roll up my spine and shoots out the top of my head.

What amazing relief! The more energy shoots into the black void, the better it feels. The plutonium-ridden orgasmic energy explodes from my crown, erupting into a giant mushroom cloud.

As the bombs in my cells explode, I experience the ultimate male orgasm, creating a burst of energy out of the top of my head, reaching high into the ethers. What a staggering amount of pulsating, intoxicated power!

I keep seeing the creation of my life, an energetic plutonium-radioactive sperm uniting with a regular egg. The absolute rush of war surges through my body as the bombs go off—such ecstasy.

I understand how men get off on war. I see combat from a new perspective; I experience how male and female bodies function. The job of the sperm is to propel itself out and penetrate. The function of the egg is to be anchored and to invite penetration. Male ejaculation is external—out, up, beyond the male body; the bigger, the better. The female orgasm goes within—the more profound the orgasm, the deeper inside it penetrates. We each do what we know at the cellular level.

Throughout history, men have been the significant champions of war, not women. The violence and destruction of bombs are masculine dominating, controlling energy, without the balance of the feminine—the lopsided reality we live in.

I am reminded of the movie Patton, where George C. Scott stops by the side of the road and proclaims with fervent emotion, "I love war! God help me; I do love it so. I love it more than my life."

I experienced the highest distorted male orgasmic rush, bursts of the great light of humanity's annihilation and destruction.

After the first few internal bombs explode, I say good night to my houseguest and retreat to my room. Throughout the night, internal bombs burst, and orgasms fly out the top of my head. In the morning, my houseguest asks what went on all night. To her ear, I made noises as though I was making rapturous, ravished love all night. She had nightmares about war and violence and could hardly wait to leave.

The bombs continued to explode internally for two more days as the orgasms skyrocketed out of the top of my head, igniting the cosmos.

STRIPPED TO THE BONE
2006

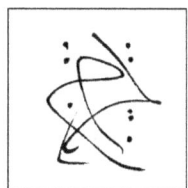

Ready to be done with the gloom and drizzle of Seattle, I sell my house and pack up everything. I place the proceeds in the stock market, along with my life savings and inheritance. The movers arrive to store my belongings while I venture into the unfamiliar, seeking my new home. But first, I head to the wilderness on a much-needed vacation.

High in the Rocky Mountains, I drive as far as my car will go on a desolate washboard dirt road and then begin to hike into the unknown. The fresh scent of pine welcomes me, twigs crackle under my feet. Aspens rustle in the breeze as the sun disappears behind the peaks. I find a flat spot nestled in the trees and quickly pitch my tent.

My first night in the wilds is blank, starless. Bushes rustle. A branch snaps. The earth trembles. I don't dare make a move; I'm alone in bear country. My mind races, every inch of me alert, ready for action. Fur bristles against the side and top of my tent. The bulge reveals an enormous, rounded body. My heart pounding, barely breathing, eyes and ears straining, poised for danger. Alert, listening. What seems like an eternity, but about five minutes later, I hear "moo." It's a frigging cow. In the morning, I wake up to a gross cow patty outside my tent. Later, I learned that ranchers graze their cattle for free on the Forest Service public land.

After a few days in the wilderness, I emerge to discover all my money is gone. Hit by the first wave of stock market debacles in 2006, at the time, I believe it is my fault. I read all the finance books; I spent $20,000 taking courses about investing money and how to increase my wealth. I followed the advice of my financial advisor, did what the old paradigm told me to do.

All our money came from bombs, destroying nature, and massive killings. I wanted nothing to do with it, and now it's all gone—my years of hard work vanish in an instant.

The following week the storage company notifies me that almost everything I own is stolen. I feel like a total failure. I'm sure I am the one to blame. Something inside me must be really wrong, dysfunctional, or even deformed. Shocked to the core, I don't know what to do. Two weeks ago, my life was great. Terror reverberates through my body—tears stream.

This isn't what I planned my life to look like at sixty. I'm so embarrassed I don't want anyone to see me. How can an intelligent woman with a Ph.D., well-traveled, expert in her field, be penniless, homeless, in massive physical pain, in a place where I knew no one?

I escape to my tent, hidden in the deep wilderness. When I received all those shots years ago, I assumed the radiation was gone, healed. Now, radiation seeps from my bones; the sensation flips between raging fires and brutal cold; either way obliterates my ability to sleep. Fireworks mixed with pins and needles explode from my neck down my spine. Sparklers crackle up and down my spine, followed by waves of raging heat and icy cold. My head is cranked tighter and tighter in a vice of radioactive energy. Plutonium has a half-life of 24,110 years, and it feels like I've been working with this pain for that long. It seems to be a never-ending process as more toxic layers release from the depths of my bones.

My life, as I have known it, is dying. Vast chunks of me dissolve and drop away as the days pass. Some days I am in death's grip. All I can do is lay on the ground and surrender. I drive to the park to walk

Cosmic Inner Seeing

along the river, and hours later, I'm still sitting behind the steering wheel of my car, unable to move.

I'm a bag lady, pushing my cart through the discounted isles in the grocery store, rummaging around in the dumpster for food, racking up my credit card bill. The Ph.D. that had a thriving practice, changing people's lives, is an imposter, a charade. The despicable, unworthy, wretched me must be the real me. I'm penniless, worthless; I have no value.

The weight of guilt and shame of my existence crush my ability to move. The shame I carry of my father's legacy runs deep, beyond mental constructs, in my unconscious and DNA.

Dirty money feeds the war, violence, and corruption of the world. I want nothing to do with it. Flames creep up my spine. My body quivers. I flashback to a marketing seminar where the man told us how to become millionaires. I don't remember what he said; I wanted to puke, got dizzy, and had to put my head in my lap so I wouldn't fall off my chair. I looked at the three hundred people in the room, none phased, each taking notes, nodding their head, and agreeing with what he spoke. I was stunned. Why don't people see what's going on underneath the surface?

I knew I had my hand in creating this mess, but lost in the vast unknown; I couldn't see my way out. I was confused about what was me and the toxic fear; I wanted to kill the inner tormentors. The only option looked like suicide.

I've contemplated suicide for decades, an unspoken voice hiding in my brain, lurking in my subconscious, wound around my DNA. Suicide, a taboo topic, is not open for discussion or inquiry. I've been chewing on the details of my demise for years. A lifetime of pain is too much to bear. I don't want to be rescued; I don't want to be found. I don't want to leave a mess for someone else to clean up. I've made my plan. Everything I need is in the trunk of my car. The final preparations are underway; today is the day to end the horrors of this life.

A deep rumbling voice irrupts from my guts, 'Choose gratitude.' What the fuck do I have to be that thankful for, my mind responds. My brain and guts are having a dialogue, more like a screaming match. My guts bellow, 'Choose gratitude.' My mind insists, 'Be done, complete, end the pain, I've had enough.'

And then I remember years ago sitting in a tiny cave in India. An inkling of the ecstatic bliss I experienced in that rock shelter drips into my heart. My heart opens, struggle dissolves. Awe washes over me. What do I have to lose if gratitude doesn't work? Nothing. And besides, I can always kill myself later.

I commit to choosing gratitude, no matter what. I start slowly. Thanks for something to eat today. Thanks for my sleeping bag. Thanks for my tent. Small baby steps.

My campfire crackles, moonbeams slice through the aspens. What in me is so messed up that I deserve this? Hot embers glow, smoke curls up, the warmth of the fire soothes my soul. Here I am, hiding in the wilds, a financial failure. Sparks fly as a log crumbles in the fire. A wave of smoke chokes my eyes. I've been in financial ruin before, but never at this depth of being homeless. An animal scurries in the brush, the stars twinkle. My mind is struggling and searching for the correct structure to move forward in. A pack of wolves howls in the distance.

One evening I'm sitting in my car watching the sunset high on a cliff—a sweeping vista in front of me, each side canyon lined with mountains. Billowing gray storm clouds roll in. Thunder rumbles, lightning strikes one side of the canyon. A few moments later, a response comes from the other side, a different rumbling with light flashes. Back-and-forth, the boom spoke, the chorus a reply. I've never witnessed anything like this before. I'm curious about what the messages convey. After half an hour, the conversation is complete. The clouds disperse, ink sky sparkles with far-reaching galaxies, star families reveal messages according to their position in the sky.

I've been hiding in the wilds for two months, scraping by. Leaves crackle, branches snap, there's a deep chill in the air. The brilliant colors of fall turn into brown mulch carpeting the earth. Winter is beckoning; hunting season starts in two days; I need a place to stay. I don't want to get shot by some drunk hunter.

RADICAL GRATITUDE
2006

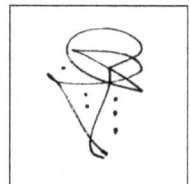

Early morning mist dissolves as I drive down the mountain to an empty laundromat at the town's edge. I scrape around for enough coins to wash and dry a load of clothes. The laundromat bathroom sink serves me well; I wash my hair and sponge bathe my body.

In my stylish, pink, perky blouse, I don the façade of Dr. Miller and offer my services at the Women's Resource Center. Much to my surprise, at the end of my talk with the executive director, she asked, "What can we do for you?"

I reply, "I'm looking for a housesitting job while writing a book." It's all true, but the wild, penniless tent woman would not have cut it. Luckily, the well-polished, educated, smart me is seen, not the homeless bag lady.

Two days later, my cell phone rang. Can I house-sit and take care of a dog for one month? Excited beyond relief, I scrub every inch of my car to perfection and hide all evidence that it's my home. I drive to a fantastic home high in the mountains with an empty car and a stuffed trunk.

Strangers in Durango welcome me and open their hearts and home. After housesitting for a month while they tour Europe, they invite me to stay at their beautiful, enormous home. I moved from a tent into a multi-million-dollar mansion. My personal living space includes a fully equipped kitchen, a living-dining area, three bedrooms, and two bathrooms. I found a job and set up payment plans with the credit card companies.

The moving company found some of my furniture and shipped it to Durango. A moving truck pulls up to a rented storage unit. The driver slinks out of the cab, hunkers down beside the truck's front wheel, looks from side to side, and grabs my cash. Sheets of paper in hand, I have the moving company's list of my belongings. The driver unpacks a few sticks of furniture and some beat-up boxes, and tells me that's it. The vast inside of the truck has areas of furniture roped off, but none of it is mine. I protest; he drives off.

After nine months, I have enough strings of my life pulled back together to get a place and function on my own. Greasy boot prints stomped on the top of my dresser, tabletops with no legs, no chairs, every box another layer of defilement. It's hard to be thankful for what I see scattered around the floor. A slow process evolves of reclaiming my dignity, releasing another layer of the ransacking of my possessions.

I'm an immaculate packer, everything precisely arranged like a work of art. Opening a box is like unwrapping a Christmas present; love and joy exude. Everything in each box goes together and tells a story of beauty, art, and love. Each item fitted in with perfection, never a broken glass, squished item, or damaged piece. After seventy-nine moves and numerous trips around the world, I'm a master at the art of packing.

A cookbook mixed with staples and paper clips, a red pair of silk panties, a potholder, and one broken cup in the same box is heartbreaking. Each box was a violation, squished coffee cups, broken bits of my grandmother's favorite vase, my possessions pillaged and plundered.

My wounds fester and deepen. Shame spreads; it's my fault; maybe I'm not good enough. Perhaps I'm not worthy enough to own beautiful things. I should've known better.

Weapons-grade plutonium 239 is man-made and has a hard shell of arrogance that's difficult to crack open. When gratitude is spinning at a very high velocity and frequency, then it will break through the hard, egotistical man-made shell, so that the plutonium-239 can be transformed. The process of breaking apart, a splitting of the atom, is something I inherited from my Dad.

And yet, true to my self-commitment, I continue using gratitude.

Spiraling Gratitude

Thanks for stealing my silver, my fork in mid-air. The cheap, well-scrubbed garage sale fork is a bit gritty and dull. Not the smoothness of my grandmother's beautiful sterling silver fork with a graceful line embossed along the handle's edge. I'm pissed.

I'm almost screaming as if someone is in front of me, shaking my fork. Thanks for stealing my fork, not a shred of gratitude or thanks.

Thank you for stealing my fork; my breathing deepens. The fork is in front of my face, trembling.

Thank you for stealing my fork. An opening occurs, tension runs out of my toes, hurt and pain puddle around my feet, and seep through the carpet, into the earth. Violation and hurt start to dissolve.

Thank you for stealing my fork. A new insight arises. The stolen fork is full of radiation. With every bite, someone is shoveling plutonium radiation into their body.

Thank you for stealing my fork—genuine thanks and blessings. I'm not poisoning myself anymore.

Thank you for stealing my fork. Instead of rage and anger, I'm heartbroken that someone is eating with radioactive silverware.

Sterling flatware for twelve people was my grandmother's, passed down to my Mom, and then to me. I used it every day. The energetic frequency of radiation Dad brought home throughout my childhood was connected to the heavy metal of the silverware.

My grandfather and great-grandfather were incredible jewelers—my treasured family heirlooms, exquisite jewelry, gone. Then I realized that the gold and silver filled with nuclear radiation's imprint could no longer poison me.

Choosing gratitude, no matter what looked and seemed crazy at times, but I was dedicated to experiencing gratitude rather than pain. I spent months on the couch, exploring the process of spiraling gratitude.

Light streams in the living room windows; I'm sprawled on the sage green velvet sofa, calling in spirals of gratitude around the radioactive sparklers zapping the back of my neck. The gazillions of shots during chelation removed most of the radiation, now it's dripping out of my bones, the next layer to be released. Sharp pains turn dull while gratitude spirals become an infinity symbol, looping between my occiput's right and left sides, connecting my brain's disassociated parts. Old patterns slide down my neck, cascade through my heart like a waterfall, and ooze out my toes. A few moments of luxurious pleasures caress my cells before the next onslaught of radioactivity fires up.

Man-made weapons-grade plutonium has a repulsive coating of conceit, audacity, and egotism not found in nature. Like cracking a hazelnut, it's hard to get through the thick shell of insolence, violence, and greed. The chipped-away hard surface falls apart, and then spirals of gratitude cut the molecule, or the energy, in two.

Imagine wrapping a piece of thread around a marshmallow and pulling it tight. The marshmallow squishes in the middle and then breaks in half. Gratitude splits apart the particle of radiation in two, revealing destruction and light. The destruction leaves my body; the light ignites more transformation. Revealing how gratitude works at the cellular level, I jot down notes daily, discovering the nuances of giving thanks.

How do I dare thank the radiation that tormented me in my entire life? How can I have gratitude for bombs destroying the Earth, annihilating people, and spreading fear and terror? How can I let go of that depth of trauma?

Drilling deep into the war in my body, I ran across the weapons-grade plutonium energy. The frequency of one hundred thirty-one nuclear explosions brought home by my Dad is imprinted in every cell. Even toxic weapons-grade plutonium can't survive in the energy field of love and gratitude.

How do we thank the unthinkable, despicable horror? Some people believe they need to remember it so that it won't happen again, but the cellular memory passes the violence down in the lineage. We've been pushing hard to survive for eons. We can evolve to a higher frequency beyond the inner struggle of fear. It starts by transforming the low frequencies with spirals of gratitude and love.

The majestic evening energy pulls me outside and down the street; music ripples through the darkness. Fire spinners practice on my neighbor's lawn, swirling flames create magical patterns in the night sky. Every week I take photos.

A gap in time occurs between when I press the button and the click of the shutter. During the camera gap, magical synchronicity is taking place. Photos uploaded to my computer at home, everything I've been writing about all week shows up in the pictures—spirals of gratitude, gratitude stitches, infinity loops.

Back on the couch, frozen trauma dissolves. The bone-chilling cold has me curled up on the sofa like a fetus, hiding under massive blankets. Spiraling gratitude dissolves the frozen trauma. Beneath or under the headaches and pain live the stark fear, rampant panic, and frozen immobilization caused by toxicity. The depth of terror, self-hatred, and annihilation that I know so well goes all the way down through my bones into the subatomic particles and DNA. After about half an hour, my body warms up. The next day, walking along the river, I stop and take photos. At home, on the computer, the images reveal a frozen face in the river.

The message is clear: create a photo book to explain how gratitude works. In 2008, I published *The Art of Radical Gratitude*. Transforming the electroshock started the development of the Gratitude Tool Kit. At each layer of pain, a new tool reveals how to change my body's energetic structures.

A more profound pain remains, but the electroshock vanishes in the high frequency of gratitude. Sixty years of stabbing neck pain melted, nightmares dissolved, and my hypoglycemia diminished. My self-hatred dwindled. The high frequency of gratitude transformed this toxic energy; I embrace it all: the good, the bad, and the unacceptable.

I gained power from death and loss, the clarity of the unchangeable, and the changeable. I gained strength emerging from the darkness and an unspoken understanding of the dark void's mysteries. I'm floating down a dark tunnel through layers of death; fear drops away as I surrender and relax. The truth of who I am is untouched.

Diving into internal terror and the depths of darkness, I corkscrew my way into the light. This is the direct opposite of going out the top of my head through meditation, prayer, or out-of-body experiences. When I follow the patriarchal tradition out of the top of my head, I leave my body behind. Like looting an abandoned store, the gremlins come in and steal my delicious, feminine life-force energy.

Courageous enough to brave the descent into the unknown void of shame, guilt, rage, and horror, I burst into joyous freedom. And then, I retreat again into the darkness and break out, through another portal, into the dazzling light—a continual process of illuminating my inner shadows. Effervescent delight bubbles up from inside; I glimpse and taste a bite of freedom.

Every day, gratitude weaves deeper into my body, transforming rage and pain into caring and love.

I wonder what would have happened if I had known about radical gratitude when fear and gremlins took over my mind after returning from India. Could my year of not being able to speak be avoided by this simple, powerful technology? How would my life be different if I had known about radical gratitude decades earlier?

THE RADIANCE PROJECT
2009

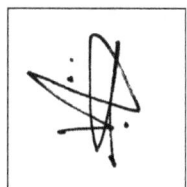

Popcorn eaten, the movie is over, the DVD self-ejects from my computer, and the screensaver, like Morse code, starts sending messages. Images of bomb photos, my art, and flowers from my book *The Art of Radical Gratitude* are displayed on my computer screen. Continual streaming, bomb certificates, my art, exploding bombs, flowers. My friend and I noticed the similarity between my art and bombs.

The next day, I arranged photos of the bombs my Dad watched explode with the art I created during chelation when radiation flowed out of my hands, squished, and oozed paint onto paper. I added the photos I took of flowers while using gratitude to heal the radiation in my body. Everything comes together; The Radiance Project is born.

On the Internet, I discovered facts about each bomb. The information corresponds to my journal entries written while creating the art; the bombs, my art, and my journal entries all line up. I made the art ten years before I found the photos of my Dad's bombs on the Internet. I had no external information; my internal knowing guided my art and my path. The depth of precise trauma wired in our bodies is mind-blowing. We all carry this level of inner knowledge.

Shockwaves surge through my body while creating one piece of art. I draw a gold circle, and years later, I realize this is the island that evaporated when bombed to smithereens.

Photos of exploding fireworks, the last piece added when I moved to Mexico. San Miguel de Allende, named after Archangel Michael, holds a fantastic three-day birthday celebration with parades and fireworks. Starting at 4 AM on Saturday, light versus dark, and good versus evil battle it out in the plaza. Fireworks stream horizontally, and masses of people gather, holding cardboard over their heads so their hair won't catch fire. Booming bottle rockets resound through town—Saturday and Sunday evenings, magnificent fireworks light the sky, beyond anything I've ever seen before, all celebrating Archangel Michael's birthday.

I upload my photos at home, and the final pieces of The Radiance Project come together. Instead of bombs, magnificent fireworks celebrate life.

The Radiance Project is a call to use the burst of light and energy from past nuclear bombs to awaken peace and radiance. The journey from war, terror, and pain through gratitude awakens change; this is my story. It's also our collective story of radiation, war, and fear that affects all of us, no matter where we live. In the combat zone or suburbia, the tremor reverberates worldwide.

Timeline:

I am the daughter of a man who not only was in charge of the building but was also there to watch 131 atomic and hydrogen bombs explode.

1995 - I'm diagnosed with weapons-grade plutonium radiation poisoning. For my treatment, I received over one hundred shots every week for one and a half years. In the night, colors pound through my body, and for the first time, I start to paint. Tremendous energy wells up, pulsates, and surges through my body, shooting out my hands. I squish and ooze cool, sensuous paint through my fingers. Mucking around in color and water, I slap, dribble, and heave paint onto the paper. Hundreds of paintings, most thrown in the trash, many stolen along with my furniture, now nine pieces of art remain. Forty to fifty years after the incidents, the frequency of bombs entwined in my body comes out in my art.

2000 - I inherit documents I call 'bomb certificates' and information about my Dad's work. I knew he built bombs, but I didn't know the extent and magnitude of destruction.

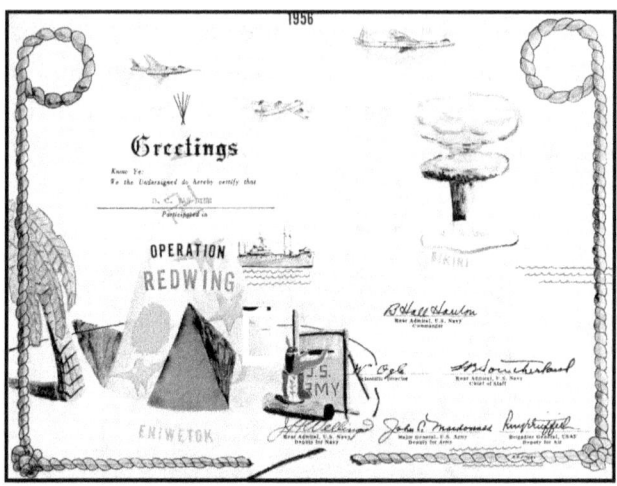

2004 - I find declassified photos on the Internet of the bombs my Dad built and watched explode.

2006 - I discovered the similarity between the bombs my father watched explode and the art I created while the radiation came out of my body.

Cosmic Inner Seeing

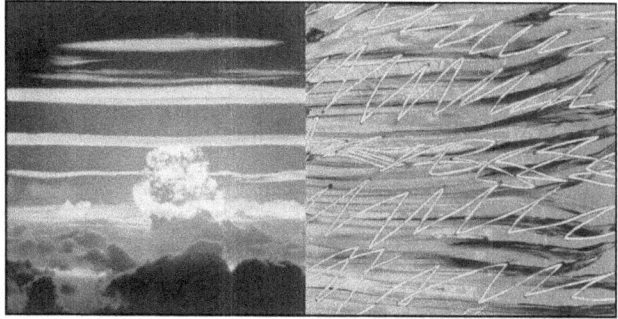

2008 - Working with gratitude to transform the radiation toxicity in my body, I created *The Art of Radical Gratitude*, a book of my photos, and the process to transform deep trauma.

2008 - I discover the connection between my art, my father's bombs, and my gratitude photos; The Radiance Project is born.

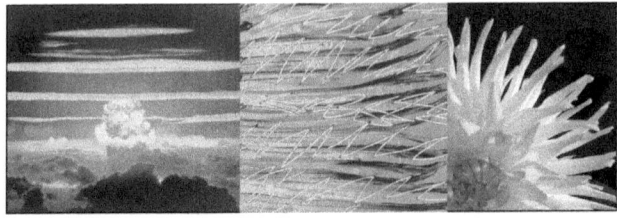

2012 - Photos from fireworks celebrating Archangel Michael's birthday in San Miguel de Allende, Mexico, are added to the Radiance Project.

From radiation to radiance, the evolution of consciousness unfolds. My lifelong vision is to transform human consciousness and create a world of love rather than violence and fear.

With a well-documented, formal grant proposal in hand, on July 25, 2010, I met with the influential global leader, Daniel Ellsberg, to discuss The Radiance Project. A few hours later, the Afghan War Diary disclosed a collection of internal U.S. military logs of the War in Afghanistan, published by WikiLeaks. Ellsberg is called to press conferences, TV interviews, and international security meetings; all thoughts of the Radiance Project vanish.

Cosmic Inner Seeing

On February 19, 2011, a friend flew to New Zealand to bring the Radiance Project to a group of art- and ecologically-minded philanthropists. On February 22, 2011, an earthquake struck Christchurch; massive devastation occurred, and all available funds were funneled to the disaster.

Not giving up, I sent a proposal to Ploughshares, an organization dedicated to reducing and eventually eliminating nuclear weapons. The day after they received my grant proposal, March 11, 2011, the Fukushima Daiichi nuclear disaster occurred. It's the most severe nuclear accident since Chernobyl, an international atomic event.

Heartbroken, I stopped all efforts related to promoting The Radiance Project.

I dive in deeper.

My life trajectory ignited when I was five years old, when my Dad exploded the world's first hydrogen bomb.

DR. CYNTHIA MILLER

What in the human psyche is so convoluted and distorted to cause such global destruction and violence?

How do we evolve beyond killing each other into joy, harmony, and peace?

What are the internal mechanisms?

HIBAKUSHA
2012 - 13

Atomic Bomb survivors are referred to in Japanese as Hibakusha, which translates literally as "bomb-affected people."

Wrought-iron benches surround the perimeter and gardens of the zocalo in the center of town; the Jardin is the meeting place in San Miguel de Allende, Mexico. In front of the seats, the Parroquia stands tall, a cross between a cathedral and a drip sandcastle covered in pink frosting. Robert is smiling, wearing a bright blue shirt and sandals; he fits in perfectly, his New York City clothes stowed in his room.

A mutual friend arranged for Robert Croonquist, founder of Hibakusha Stories, and me to meet. Over lunch, I learn about his program to bring survivors of the bombing of Hiroshima and Nagasaki to share their stories with New York City high school students. Robert's warm, loving smile brings ease and safety to the conversation. Hibakusha Stories' primary focus is to highlight the testimony of Hiroshima and Nagasaki survivors and use that inspiration to take action for disarmament to create a peaceful and sustainable world.

I tell my story about my Dad building bombs, pain, and sickness, and my desire for peace and global change. At the end of lunch, he invited me to New York City to meet the bomb survivors in May 2012, nine months from now.

One month before my trip, I received the schedule. I'm so scared I throw up for a week. How can I meet these heroic survivors of the bomb? A week later, I found out they all are from Hiroshima. Tears flow for days. In a few weeks, I'll be meeting three survivors of the bombing of Hiroshima. The image of my carrying the souls of these women's families and friends haunts me. Do I dare tell them? What will people think if I share my experience? Will I be made wrong, disbelieved, or dismissed? What will happen if I speak up?

Distraught, I pace back and forth between my cool living room couch and the sunny wrought-iron chair nestled between red and fuchsia bougainvillea. I'm anxious and shaky.

New York City is foreign and a bit frightening. I live in historic San Miguel with cobblestone streets, no stoplights in Centro, and sidewalks almost wide enough for one person. Friends stop on the street, give me a hug and a kiss on the cheek. A slow-paced life, beauty abounds, doorways open to magical gardens, and red, fuchsia, and orange bougainvilleas drip over courtyard walls, gracing the streets.

The intensity and density of NYC are daunting. Horns, sirens, and multiple languages collide. Fast-moving crowds talking on cell phones jockey along wide cement sidewalks, neon lights flash, buildings engulf the sky.

Robert meets me in Chelsea; we taxi to Dr. Kathleen Sullivan, Hibakusha Stories Director's lovely home. On the second-floor landing, piles of shoes and a basket of slippers wait by the door. Inside is an open floor plan where the gracious living, dining, and kitchen merge into one space. About fifteen people mill about chatting and fixing food.

I'm so nervous it is hard to breathe. Beautiful Shigeko is the first to greet me; she takes my hands, "Welcome, please don't feel respon-

Cosmic Inner Seeing

sible for what your father did." Her eyes sparkle, and her smile radiates. The room, filled with generosity, is a safe container for each of us to be held in love. Relieved, I met everyone.

Every day I'm paired with a different Hibakusha to visit two high schools to tell our stories. I hear their stories for the first time while sitting on stage. Before me are hundreds of restless street-smart teenagers. Terror grips my body, trained to keep quiet since childhood, especially about bombs; public speaking is not my forte.

Toshiko Tanaka was six when the bomb dropped. "I looked up to the sky; I was attacked by the high heat rays and blinded by the flash. I covered my face with my right arm, so I got severe burns on my right arm, head, and left neck. I could not understand what happened. It was pitch dark around me, caused by the dust of the bomb blast contaminated by radioactivity, called an atomic cloud. Soon I felt the severe pain of my burned skin."

Shigeko Sasamori looked up to see a plane flying overhead and was knocked unconscious by the blast. Unrecognizable from the burns on her face and body, thirteen-year-old Shigeko cried out for water, repeating her name and address. After four days and nights calling out for help, she finally reunited with her family.

Reiko Yamada spoke of her experience. One part that hit me was, "A good friend of mine was waiting for her mother to return home. On the second day after the bombing, a moving black lump crawled into the house. They first thought it was a black dog, but they soon realized it was their mother; she collapsed and died at her children's feet. They cremated her body in the yard."

Guts churning, almost dizzy, choked up, and on the verge of tears, I stand on the stage and say, "My father built that bomb." Half asleep, students sit up straight, eyes wide open, amazed. This wrenching process happens twice a day for ten days.

At Jamaica High School, everyone passes through security clearance, like the airport. I place my purse on the conveyor belt that radiates my stuff, scanning for guns and knives. Then I walk through the frame of the metal detector. These brilliant students have a daily dose of radiation to their brains, bodies, and the food they bring to school.

DR. CYNTHIA MILLER

I'm shocked that the students have to endure this continuous radiation exposure.

That day I'm paired with Toshiko, a wonderful sweet artist who still resides in Hiroshima. We sit in the taxi's back seat heading to the next school. A heavy metallic taste bites my tongue, and sharp radiation eats my teeth.

"Toshiko, do you feel radiation drip down your gums?" I ask.

Robert, sitting in the front seat, whips his head around in shock and says. "I've never heard of such a thing."

"Oh yes, radiation dripped from my teeth but stopped when I was twenty," Toshiko answers.

After a moment of reflection, Toshiko adds, "As part of the peace treaty, the government prohibited us from talking about how the radiation affected our bodies. At the clinic, Hibakusha was observed, measured, and quantified, but never treated."

"I wasn't allowed to talk about it either; everything in our home was top-secret." For decades doctors disregarded me when I brought up radiation as a possible cause for my pain.

Shigeko Sasamori, Reiko Yamada, Toshiko Tanaka, and me.

Spiral steps lead to a Chelsea brownstone's second floor, opening to a large bright rectangular room, the windows on each end float up to high ceilings. Sliding wooden panels with glass separate the living from the dining room. An ornate mirror above the mantle reflects light throughout the room.

Hibakusha, interpreters, volunteers, and hosts sit around the table. White chopsticks in hand, halfway through dinner, I start shaking, I feel like I'll explode; I can't hold it in anymore. I blurt out my story about taking on the souls of Hiroshima when I was a fetus.

I watch emotions, like different colors of paint, fly across the Japanese women's faces. One of the female hosts skillfully changes the subject. In private, the survivors come to me and acknowledge my story. Souls are an integral part of Japanese culture and tradition. Relief surges through my body, stories I've heard from the Hibakusha confirm my inner knowing and hidden experience.

I'm with Shigeko *Sasamori, wearing the kimono she gave me.*

The next year I return to New York City. Many of my friends from last year are here. During our welcome gathering, Shigeko gives me a blue and white full-length kimono. She has me put it on and shows me how to tie the bright yellow obi around my waist. After giving me a big hug and saying, "Welcome to the family," I feel loved, acknowledged, and seen.

We are joined by Yasuaki Yamashita from Nagasaki, along with Clifton Truman Daniel, President Truman's grandson. President Truman signed the bill to drop the bombs on Japan.

Clifton Truman Daniel, Shigeko Sasamori, me, Yasuaki Yamashita at the Japan Society

I'm all choked up at the Japan Society in New York City; we are on stage in front of hundreds of people and simultaneously broadcast to Japan. I apologize to the Japanese for the bombings and my father's role in the destruction.

On the last school visit of the trip, I was on stage at a high school with two others, Shigeko Sasamori and Clifton Truman Daniel. I saw an arch or energy circle around the room as we spoke. Some level of global healing transpired, completing the cycle.

That night, at the American bistro Cafe Loup in Manhattan, we are one big happy family, laughing, tasting each other's dinners, and sharing desserts. Joy and glee fill the room. As we are leaving, the restaurant owner approaches me, saying, "I know the Japanese, the interpreters, and Clifton, President Truman's grandson, but who are you?" I reply, "My father built the bombs." I watched her face transform from curiosity to shock and amazement, and then a smile emerged. Her eyes beamed in recognition of the global transformation and healing taking place.

I wonder what glitch in the human psyche, what malfunction in the DNA causes people to create nuclear warfare. The question remains, how do we evolve beyond killing each other?

THE GALACTIC PETRI DISH EXPERIMENT
2017

I need help.

Panic attacks keep me stuck at home—my Post Traumatic Stress Disorder (PTSD) flares. I find a practitioner of EMDR, or Eye Movement Desensitization and Reprocessing, to assist me. During one session, I see myself as a fetus. This is the seeing I've used for years with my clients, ignited by my spontaneous Kundalini awakening. I'm an embryo, curved from head to tail, with no arms or legs yet. The sides of my neck are gills. I look more like a tadpole than a human. My spine is a ridge that elongates down to my tail. My head and spine look like I have a Mohawk haircut. Instead of hairs sticking straight up, each hair is a microscopic probe connecting me to other dimensions, times, and realms in various regions of the galaxy.

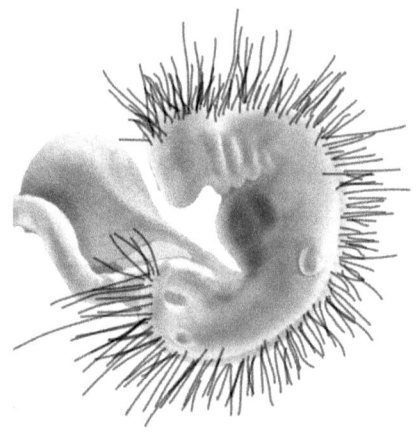

The needles start at my forehead, run along the center top of my head, and down the ridge of my forming spine. Each probe leads to a unique world of different frequencies, ranging from dark realities to unknown magical kingdoms. Each implant tests and monitors in a distinct way, making sure I survive the annihilating blast of radiation, terror, and countless obliterated souls.

I'm a cell in a cosmic Petri dish overseen by galactic scientists. Microscopic probes line up from the front of my forehead, down my spine, into my tail. I'm a six-week-old fetus, the size of a lentil, being prepared for a cosmic experiment.

My tiny fetus feels helpless at the onslaught of forces wanting to use my body for their benefit and my detriment. I'm terrified, trying to hide and escape. There is no way out. I'm held in the confines of my mother's womb, chained in with an umbilical cord. Alone, there is no safety, no one on my side, protecting and nurturing me.

There is no escaping the microscopic inserts. Each probe locks in another layer of fear and terror. Panic jammed in with each etheric pierce, embedded in my newly forming cells. Fear laced into the entire fabric of my developing nervous system. The trauma of the probes is etched into every neuron. I feel helpless in the face of this imposing dark force.

A week later, in another healing session, I noticed a slightly older fetus. This fetus has arms, legs, fingers, and toes, and my tail has disappeared. I'm assaulted with a wave, a blast of light, shock waves, and heat. Heart racing, I want to jump out of my body—a fierce light and clouds of radioactive smoke melt through my center. I feel split in two. Dismembered soul parts and DNA bits crumble together in torrents of flaming wind, billowing smoke, and radioactive shock waves, impregnating my body. Japanese souls filled with hatred towards Americans fill black clouds, crowding out my essence. The terror, raging fires, burning flesh, and vaporized bodies demand attention. Thousands of tortured souls take over my body, waging a secret war for space and tender loving care. The real me retreats into the background.

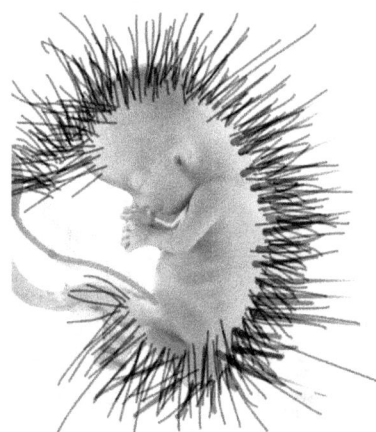

An unknown number of infinitesimal probes monitor my body. I am being checked by a vast assortment of beings across the cosmos. My body is manipulated to keep me alive. Some are beings of light; others are of the darkest sort. Everyone is curious about this experiment.

My therapist, ill-equipped to deal with this level of trauma, wanted me to put everything into an internal box and not look at it. I quit therapy and worked on my own.

I want validation. I searched online to find photos of fetal development. The images reveal my exact inner seeing. According to the pictures, I was about six weeks old when the probes were inserted. I see the bumps of my just-closed neural tube are impregnated with needles. This neural tube curves and bulges into three sections: my forebrain, midbrain, and hindbrain, and the beginnings of my spinal cord. The beginning of my nervous system is taking place. Millions of microscopic neurons connect, synapses form, and internal communication begins.

I explore Dad's records. Before my conception, Dad traveled from Hanford to Los Alamos, carrying weapons-grade plutonium-239. He also transports uranium-235 from Oak Ridge to Los Alamos. Any radiation that might have leaked during transport is known to travel to the bones and the sex cells.

Online birth charts date my conception to about May 29, Memorial Day. Travel records reveal Dad's three-day leave to go home for Memorial Weekend.

I was about six weeks old when the implants were inserted, which would be around July 10, 1945. Trinity, the world's first atomic bomb, exploded on July 16, 1945.

The next fetus I see, my tail has disappeared, I have tiny arms and legs, and I'm about one and a half inches. The online photos show this as a ten-week-old fetus. Ten weeks from my conception is August 6, 1945, the day the bomb was dropped on Hiroshima. All the dates line up. World events validate my inner seeing.

I wonder how my mother felt carrying a galactic pincushion in her womb. After I was born, we never bonded. She didn't hold me when I was a baby. Who would want to cuddle a prickly porcupine? Who would want to get near such a monstrosity? Was I so despicable that she could not love me?

Souls in agony invaded me with no regard or respect for me. I'm their enemy, to be hated and despised. I felt worthless, kicked aside like a piece of garbage.

Unconscious energetic probes, jammed into my neck and spinal column, siphon off my feminine energy, feeding the destructive male forces. I was a surrogate to be violated and trashed for male power and greed. The dark forces steal my innocent, sweet, precious nectar.

I had to shut down my power to create space for the souls. Each of the splintered-off parts feels frantic. Like a fly trying to get out of a closed glass jar, my frenetic nervous system tries to connect to other parts of my body but is blocked by the trauma. This internal splitting and fragmenting caused me to react by running away, freezing, or becoming immobilized. These are the survival mechanisms of the ancient reptilian brain. The grief, shame, and guilt are enormous. I carry my father's legacy in my DNA, bones, cells, and nervous system.

Prenatal trauma has shown up as a lifetime of headaches and incessant pain in my occiput for at least sixty years—this is the Post Traumatic Stress Disorder (PTSD) that keeps me curled up on the couch for days, immobilized, afraid to see anyone. Panic attacks—excruciating pain disrupting daily life. Pre-birth trauma is the damage that hinders my full functioning in the world and sabotages my finances and relationships.

The one hundred and fifty thousand burning, radiated, bombed souls teetering on the edge of annihilation, scream terrified for their very existence across all of space and time. If they had perished, a massive tear in the cosmic web would have disturbed the grander cosmic order.

What about me? This body is programmed for others. Am I worthless, to be used by others as a way station, a place to dump fear, radiation, pain, and suffering, and then move on? How do I care for myself? Who is there to care for me? What about this body, this nervous system, my hopes, dreams, and well-being?

Since I was a fetus, my brain development had no way to differentiate between who I was and the toxic debris of thousands of radioactive Japanese souls. It's taken tremendous digging to find myself, and then to love that tiny being who was so incredibly brave and courageous.

My body imprinted off the shattered, blown apart DNA and neural programs of Japanese trained to hate and despise Americans. My fetus formed to the frequencies of nuclear warfare, annihilating the enemy, and destroying the ecosystem. Instead of replicating that out in the world, I turned the frequencies inside into inner warfare, self-annihilation, and destroying my self-worth and value. No wonder I had such a profound lack of self-worth and depth of self-hatred.

It's been hard to get to the core of all of this. I've had to discover how to transform my own body, all the way down to my DNA. I had no one to guide the way. No one knew what I was talking about; I had to do it on my own.

It took me decades to learn how to clear the trauma that is a part of my nervous system's development. I've been working on clearing the imprints out of my neck for years. The implants were dismantled years ago, but still, the old circuitry remains. Like the fading ruins of an abandoned theme park, rusty metal and paint flakes crinkle off the carousel. I no longer choose to take on the hidden job of keeping the merry-go-round moving, the wheel of life going round and round, through fear and terror. I'm now on the side, watching.

Spirals of Radical Gratitude ignite an inner dissolving. The technologies I use with my clients help me to replace my old circuitry with the structure of my essence. The energetic goo created to keep inner factions at war, to make me feel cut off and isolated, flows out into the depths of the earth.

My essence appears in her full force and magnificence and tells the invading energies to leave. Instead of a demand, a negotiation takes place, each side claiming a part of me. The vows, contracts, and agreements set up before coming into this life are renegotiated. In the past, I've rescinded my vows, which never really worked for me. Like divorce lawyers bickering over who gets what, the outside forces proclaim, "You agreed to take on this burden, remember." My soul expands, and beautiful light radiates, evaporating the dark forces. The malevolent energy dissipates.

Cosmic Inner Seeing

I need to come to peace. Radiation and the Japanese souls impact every moment of my life. Resentment builds. According to mainstream American media, I'm a complete failure. I lost all my money. I live below the poverty line on social security. I'm so filled with trauma that I can't get it together to earn piles of cash.

If I speak up, will I be locked away, drugged up, or shocked with electrotherapy? Even though eyewitnesses were watching the soul's exodus from my body, will people call me crazy, make fun of me, or ostracize me? What if they just can't see? What if they are blind to other dimensions and realities?

The process of disconnecting from the inherited and childhood circuitry to create and morph into a new reality triggers fear. The terror is not about seeing my darkness and how wretched I am, but about seeing my magnificence. I've been programmed to be afraid of who I am. I certainly am not allowed to reveal my truth to others. The real fear is my light, my expanded self, and my gifts.

I'm expanding into a more accurate multi-dimensional version of who I am.

Finally, I see that very few people have the ability and the opportunity to do what I did, to have the experience in my body of transforming the DNA and fragments of hundreds of thousands of souls. For forty-one years, my internal alchemical process was to reunite all the DNA strands and fragments with the correct soul body—no small feat. I know the courage required to take on such a tremendous task that most people wouldn't even believe.

Things begin to make sense. I have the tools to get myself out of the mess I volunteered to take on. My spontaneous Kundalini awakening allowed me the vision to see what is happening inside bodies, mine and other people's. It took me decades of helping my clients for me to develop the necessary skills to transform my neural programs, thought patterns, and pain. I am evolving into a new human. The rigors and unusual experiences of my life are the foundation for me to help others evolve into a new reality.

The inner surge of evolution pulsates through my body, a force much more significant than my 3-D human life. Tears streaming, gasping for air, my chest rips open, and the heartbreak of humanity gushes out, exposing the entire cosmos in the core of my being. I am one with cosmic intelligence.

BOOK 3

MULTI-DIMENSIONAL AWAKENING

WEAVING THE PIECES TOGETHER
2025

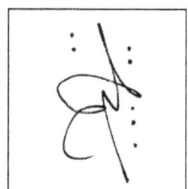

It has been five years since I published this book. The last chapters were confusing in the original version, so I've rewritten them.

When I set out to write the story of my life, it looked like a jumbled-up mess. I felt like a failure because I was so weird and didn't fit into any of the molds of Western culture. There was no framework for my wide-ranging, unusual experiences.

In the old 3-D model, I was squished and jammed into a limited structure of who I could be. It was impossible to function fully; cut off from my inner resources, I felt incomplete and unsuccessful. Everything was kept in compartments, each dimension separate, only a few revealed at a time, at various phases of my life.

Many of the things I feared, hated, or judged about myself became my superpowers, allies, and strengths. What looked like unconnected, divergent, weird experiences, when seen from a different vantage point, chart the trajectory of my life.

I've lived with the right brain knowing about multiple dimensions for over fifty years. The split-second burst of Shakti out of the top of my head during my spontaneous Kundalini awakening rewired my brain to see multiple dimensions. But I never mapped out the dimensions, gave them names, or connected them to my linear, logical left brain.

I realized that each outrageous event of my life took place in a different dimension. Exploring the bizarre, conflicting experiences, I put the puzzle pieces together and saw the tapestry of my life—and myself—in a new way. A surprise realization hit me: maybe I'm not as fucked up as I'd always thought.

Excitement arose as I explored my expansion into multiple dimensions—sorting through the old limiting programs and discovering the hidden gems was a fantastic experience. Joy bubbled up from my depths, and space to be all of me opened. Happiness and freedom rippled through my body. Finally, I had a framework to hold all the different facets of who I am.

And then, once I uncovered the first twelve dimensions, the next step was to see how I connected with each one. When I wove the dimensions together, the soul path of my life became very clear.

A New Model for Conscious Evolution

Writing about my life evolved into *Inner Evolution: Remembering Your Power*, where I charted out a new map of reality. Then the framework became alive in my body, DNA, and twelve dimensions.

The *Inner Evolution* is a radical approach to healing, transformation, and evolution. It takes you on a journey to release the patriarchy in your body, to transform feelings of being unloved, and to claim your inner authority. It's safe to let go of your wounds, previous ideas of who you're supposed to be, and what others think about you.

No more hiding, self-hatred, or lack of self-worth because you don't fit into the prescribed norm of societal expectations. Inner torment and trauma dissolve, self-love blossoms, and your life transforms.

Your life unfolds in multiple dimensions; the pleasure of embodying who you are is the most exciting adventure of a lifetime. You've waited for eons for this time. The *Inner Evolution* is a portal into a new you and reality. The new model includes a comprehensive map for the next leap in consciousness.

Are you ready to create change in your life? Unless you intervene, your life functions on unseen inner patriarchal programming that has nothing to do with the essence of who you are. Explore a new model of reality and reconstruct the unseen processes that shape your life. Uncover the magic and mystery of navigating and claiming who you are.

It's time to discover more of who you are.

IT'S YOUR TURN!
2025

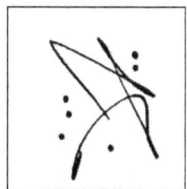

Dear Reader,

I invite you to look at your life through a new lens. I hope reading my story inspires courage and permission to explore the tales of your life. I encourage you to write down your experiences. You don't have to show it to anyone if you don't want to.

Write down all the unusual, incredible, and exciting things you've done in your life. Journal about the times you hid and the times something extraordinary happened.

Over the years, clients told me amazing stories they were too timid to mention to anyone else. The limited 3-D reality had no place to hold their life's incredible experiences. Many remained quiet because they were fearful of being disbelieved or made wrong. They buried their stories and their magnificence.

What if you're an amazing multidimensional being whose purpose is to embody your extraordinary multidimensional facets into your body? A radical concept that goes against what we've been taught.

What would your life be like if you saw yourself from a fresh vantage point and claimed the multidimensional magnificence of who you are? The profound joy and delight of multiple dimensions coming out to play is phenomenal.

Steven Pressfield wrote in *Turning Pro*, "The pain of being human is that we are all angels imprisoned in vessels of flesh." When confined to our limited 3-D neural programming, we can't embody our angelic aspects.

Being suspended between two worlds, pain, confusion, and lack of self-worth arise from the innermost depths of who we are. Our expanded multidimensional selves hold all of who we are—the angelic, the cosmic, and the human. In this state, profound safety emerges, inner pain dissolves, and joy radiates.

But fear stops us. What will people think? Will our parents, children, or friends reject us? Will we be ostracized for expressing who we are? Ingrained fears keep us stuck and in our place.

The next evolutionary step of humanity is from a limited 3-D perspective to an expanded cosmic multidimensional vision. When connected to our expanded multidimensional selves, it's a joyous celebration, with freedom to explore vast universes and uncharted territory. From this luscious place, life unfolds in mysterious ways beyond our wildest imagination. New connections arise, doors open, and we meet others along the way. Together, we co-create a new reality.

Early adopters, change-makers, and path-breakers are waiting for this map. People disillusioned and fed up with the status quo, heartbroken by humanity's current state—the visionaries who see a new reality but don't know the path.

Individually, we are creating new stories about our lives. Collectively, our unique stories are making a completely different world. The *Inner Evolution: Remembering Your Power* is a model to help map out our collective future.

Instead of squishing into a 3-D structure, can you imagine what it will be like to create a world with people connected to multiple strands of activated DNA and twelve dimensions?

There's so much inside that wants to come out—magical wisdom, wizardry, and new perceptions. The most thrilling ride of your life is the journey into the depths of you.

Exploring the depth of who you are reveals why you are on Earth at this moment. This time of profound chaos, deception, and awakening is the perfect opportunity to reinvent a new you and a better world for all. Imagine a world that celebrates who you are—your diversity, weird uniqueness, and hidden gifts are welcome.

We are on the cutting edge of a quantum leap of consciousness. What kind of world will we envision? When I look, it's beyond my imagination. I see iridescent lights and magical colors. I feel love, joy, and pleasure. Anything is possible.

What's your vision for the future? Bring your wondrous, magical love to this beautiful blue sphere. Contribute your part to create a splendid world for all. Together, we create a wonderful tapestry to birth a new reality.

I offer you the gift of my life story and a new multidimensional map of reality for your healing and evolution.

Discover more of who you are. Expand your magnificent light and create magic in the world. Are you ready to join me to evolve into deeper gratitude and love to birth a new reality?

Let's connect!
Please visit DrCynthiaMiller.com

ACKNOWLEDGMENTS

Writing this book has taken years, with multiple layers of kindness and support along the way.

I am so thankful to Barbara and Stuart Shore, the angels in Durango, Colorado, whose loving-kindness assisted me through the darkest phase of my life.

A joyous shout out to Kristin Dainis for her fantastic support and profound editing skills to help me create the best book possible to convey my message.

A huge depth of gratitude goes to the Akimbo community, Seth Godin, and Kristin Hatcher. An enormous thanks to Linda McLachlan, Diane Osgood, Nicolette Wills, Kathy Karn, Scott Perry, and Michael Feeley for holding me in a safe, generous, loving community while I birthed this book and The *Inner Evolution*. Your comments, feedback, and support cheered me on.

A heartfelt thanks to Adam Gainsburg, the originator of Soul Sign, for adding his expertise and excellent, loving support.

Thank you, Susan Page, founder of the San Miguel Writers Conference, for encouraging me to write this book.

My gratitude goes to the first writing group I was in, Florence Grende, Lynda Schor, Marcia Loy, John Scherber, Christina Johnson, and Michael Landfair. When they read my chapter on the river, they encouraged me, letting me know I could write, capture attention, and touch people's emotions. Without their encouragement, I would have stopped writing. After months of writing, my PTSD was triggered, and I had to quit the group and heal the exposed trauma.

Thanks to Laura Hollick, founder of Soul Art, and the wonderful

Soul Art community for their inspiration and loving support. During my Soul Art Certification program, Laura encouraged me to explore light codes. Light codes expanded into a multidimensional technology. Thank you, Laura, for assisting me to 'Go for the gold.'

Thanks to Francesca Fisher, owner of Los Senderos in San Miguel de Allende, Mexico, for her interest in The Radiance Project and for introducing me to Robert Croonquist.

I have incredible gratitude to Robert Croonquist of Hibakusha Stories for the depth of compassion he holds for Japan's bombing survivors. His level of love changes the world.

Thank you to all my clients for trusting me with their innermost secrets, fears, and dreams and for showing parts of themselves never exposed before. For the willingness to change, rewire their bodies, let go of fears and trauma, and live the life of their dreams. I couldn't have done this without them.

GLOSSARY

Ashram: An ashram is a spiritual hermitage or a monastery in Indian religions, or a dwelling place dedicated to spiritual pursuits.
Cell: One of the specialized units, consisting of the nucleus and protoplasm, composes the bodies of plants and animals. The primary activity of all cells is to transform energy.
Chakra: A Hindu term for a spiritual energy center just outside but connected to the physical body.
Corpus Callosum: The corpus callosum is the arched bridge of nervous tissue that connects the two cerebral hemispheres, allowing communication between the right and left sides of the brain.
Critical Mass: The minimum mass of fissionable material, which can sustain a chain reaction.
Evolution: Changes in the genetic composition of a population during successive generations. The gradual development of more complex organisms from smaller, more simple ones.
Frequency: The number of completed cycles, waves, vibrations, etc., of a periodic phenomenon per second.
Hibakusha: Hibakusha, a person affected by exposure to a bomb, is a Japanese word generally designating the people affected by Hiroshima and Nagasaki's 1945 atomic bombings.

Glossary

Ida: The white, lunar left subtle psychic channel or Nadi coiling around the Sushumna and ending at the left nostril.

Kali: The Divine Shakti, representing the creative and destructive aspects of nature. Kali is the symbol of the dynamic power of eternal time, and in this aspect, she signifies annihilation through which the seed of life emerges. She inspires terror and love at the same time.

Karma: The Hindu and Buddhist philosophy, according to which their behavior in this life determines the quality of people's current and future lives.

Kriya: Kriya is the path of action, a specific movement of the body.

Kundalini: A powerful spiritual energy usually lying dormant in the physical body at the spine's base. Once carefully awakened, spiritual growth ensues.

Light Codes are like snowflakes; no two are the same; they stream in from different dimensions and source. Magical packets of information, or quanta, light codes, like Pac-Man, eat the old toxic waste. They also bring in high-frequency information necessary for your evolution and transformation.

Limbic System: the Limbic System is in the middle part of the brain and is involved in human emotion regulation; it is concerned with emotions and instincts, feeding, and dogmatic and paranoid tendencies.

Linga: A stylized phallus, used to represent the Hindu god Shiva. Exoteric meaning, phallus, esoteric meaning, subtle space in which the whole universe is in the process of formation and dissolution.

Mudra: A mudra is a sacred finger movement; yogic control of specific organs helps concentration, which produces psychic responses.

Neocortex: The neocortex is the newest part of the brain and is concerned with speech, rational thought, and problem-solving. It also affects creativity and the ability to learn.

Paradigm: A scientific model that offers a system by which events in the field can be explained better than they can be by existing models, is sufficiently open-ended to leave all sorts of problems resolved—a model or map of perceived reality.

Pingala: The subtle solar channel on the right side of the body, coiling around the Sushumna.

Prana: A Hindu or yogic term used to describe the life force.

Quantum: Quanta, a discrete "packet" or unit of energy, angular momentum, or other physical quantities, representing a minimum, indivisible quantity.

Reptilian Brain: The reptilian brain acts on stimulus and response, is fear-driven, and is the oldest part of the brain.

Samadhi: The deep meditation, trance, superconscious state in which identification is realized: the final goal of yoga.

Shakti: Shakti is the Sanskrit term of the feminine energy of the divine. It is a Hindu term for the energy that passes through the Chakras and is stored at the spine's base. Shakti is the dynamic aspect of the Ultimate Principle, the power that permeates all creation, the foundational consciousness's energy.

Shiva (Siva): Hindu god. In esoteric meaning, Siva is Pure Consciousness, the transcendent divine principle.

Shiva-Linga: A stone form that symbolizes the totality in which the male and female principles are eternally united.

Spiraling Radical Gratitude: A process to shift lower energies by bringing in the high frequencies of gratitude and love.

Sushumna: The subtle channel in the center of the spinal column through which the Kundalini rises.

Vibration: Vibrating motion or one unit of this, being a complete motion from a middle point out to one limit, then back through the central point to the other and back to the starting point again.

Wave: A time-varying quantity, which is also a function of position.

ABOUT THE AUTHOR

Dr. Cynthia Miller is a visionary, alchemist, and evolutionary change agent dedicated to catalyzing a profound shift in human consciousness. Her work centers on rewiring neural pathways, transforming DNA, and elevating the frequency of individuals and the collective. She is here to help birth a new inner neurological reality, a major step in humanity's evolution.

She has developed groundbreaking, multidimensional technologies for over four decades to guide thousands toward personal transformation, self-worth, and fulfillment.

Her revolutionary framework, *Inner Evolution*, provides a multidimensional map for shifting from fear and suffering to awakening, safety, and love.

A mystic storyteller, Dr. Miller shares her wisdom through her books, including *Inner Evolution: Remembering Your Power*, *The Art of Radical Gratitude*, and *I Am Worthy: Ignite Your Feminine Power*—a self-help adult coloring book designed to inspire empowerment.

Dr. Cynthia Miller's mission is clear: When enough individuals awaken and rewire their inner world, humanity and reality will transform.

DrCynthiaMiller.com

Read about new insights and breakthroughs in
the *Inner Evolution Substack Publication*.
https://theinnerrevolution.substack.com/

www.ingramcontent.com/pod-product-compliance
Lightning Source LLC
Chambersburg PA
CBHW071903290426
44110CB00013B/1262